Garden Thoughts

Marta Kastner

Illustrations by Dorothy Blackwell

Cedar Hill Press
2004

to Max – a Gardener!

Marta Kastner

2-16-'19

Contents

HOW IT STARTED

I came to gardening on my own, relatively late in life. Earlier it just did not come up. Most of the year I lived in the city, garden was part of the summer - and someone else's responsibility.

Neither of my parents ever planted a radish or pulled a weed, and probably could not tell which was which. Their parents were not much better, although in later years my maternal grandmother tried to imitate her brothers, who were both gardeners, and started a rock garden, with indifferent success. The best gardener in the family was my great grandfather but he died before I was born.

Gardens were something you went to see as part of historic or famous houses. The interest was more architectural than horticultural.

It was not until I moved to California, where when you put a stick into ground, next month there is a bush, that the gardening bug bit me. I thought it miraculous that huge plants can grow from such small and insignificant seeds - and frankly I still do.

What I like about gardening is that it is a microcosm of life; unpredictable and often perverse, but never, never boring.

GARDENS PLAIN AND FANCY

My garden is in the Valley of Virginia, more or less at the end of it. To be precise just east of Lexington, south of Buena Vista and north of Natural Bridge. The early 19c farm house faces the Blue Ridge Mountains which offer a magnificent panorama year round, unless it gets foggy. The Alleghenies can be glimpsed if you climb into the attic and crane your neck.

It is a good gardening country. The soil is mostly clay, but fertile, and usually there is enough rain. The winters are seldom very cold nor are the summers too hot. Most everybody here gardens, whether they live in town or in the country, and I am in awe of their expertise.

It was always thus. The gardening tradition started in the 1770s when Thomas Jefferson planned his magnificent garden at Monticello. He was a true blue gardener and his garden notes are full of interesting bits of information, dates when seeds were sown or stuff harvested. Also a great deal about the costs. Which is not surprising. As we know all his life Jefferson suffered from financial dilemmas.

Although we may not think of him in that way, Thomas Jefferson was a farmer and depended on crops for his income. By the end of the century he had 10,800 acres of land under cultivation, some of this in Rockbridge county, where I live. But he was also a pleasure gardener

growing many of the flowers that we still plant and enjoy.

In no way do I see myself in the same class as Jefferson, but closer to home there is another Thomas with whom I can identify. This is Thomas Jackson, usually known as Stonewall. In the 1850s, before he became a famous Confederate general, he had his one and only home in Lexington. And he too was a gardener, but, for the record, the name Stonewall had absolutely nothing to do with any stone walls in any garden.

Shortly after I moved to Rockbridge county I joined the Stonewall Jackson House as a docent. Over the years I became quite familiar with Jackson's garden because the museum has recreated it very much as it was in his day. Luckily he too left us a record of what he was growing.

His is not a large garden, only a few feet wider than the house and not very deep, in all about a quarter of an acre. But Jackson grew many things there. It was mostly vegetables but also flowers and there were several fruit trees that came with the house. One of them was an apricot tree. I wonder whether he had many apricots. I have three apricot trees which usually get nipped by frost while blooming so I hardly ever get any fruit.

Jackson also grew cabbages, carrots, turnips, potatoes, celery and other things. The celery intrigued me and one year I decided to do the same both at home and in Jackson's garden. It was harder than I expected, and I fear my celery was in no competition to his. The secret is in hilling it to keep the stalks pale and blanched - which I failed to do. So the result were short, dark green stalks with an intense taste. They were not much good for munching but worked well for seasoning of stock and stews.

Jackson also grew tomatoes. In one of his letters he mentioned that he was helping their old cook to can them. This was so typical of him. I am quite sure there wasn't another gentleman in Lexington who worked alongside his slaves hoeing or harvesting his crops, and then in the evening came into the kitchen to can tomatoes and corn.

But Jackson always said, "Determine what is the right thing to do and do it" - and he did. This was a fine advice then and still is today.

GARDENER'S YEAR

I had an uncle, a grand uncle actually, who was a gardener. Many years ago he wrote a book called "The Gardener's Year." This book, I suppose, is a small offering to his memory.

His name was Karel Capek, (pronounced Chapek), and he was a brother of my maternal grandmother. "The Gardener's Year" was not his magnum opus. He wrote other books, plays and newspapers articles, as one of the leading writers in Czechoslovakia of the post World War I. generation. He is still read in Europe, but in the United States he is known only by a few as librettist of "The Makropoulos Secret," an opera by Leos Janacek, and perhaps as author of a play RUR, where for the first time appears the word "robot".

Makropoulos is about a woman who has the secret of eternal youth, which as you can imagine, turns out to be a rocky pleasure, and eventually at the end of her first 300 years she decides it is not worth the trouble. But while it lasts she has a good run. Several years ago, when it was presented at the Metropolitan Opera, a member of the cast suffered a heart attack in the opening scene and died. This made the story even more poignant.

RUR, or to give it its full name, Rossum's Universal Robots goes on another tack, to future. It is a satire on industrial materialism, the human race slowly dying out, robots taking over, but also a new beginning for the world as a robot couple subtly becomes human. The 'robot' came from a Czech word for hard labor. When I was teaching I would mention the origin of robot to my students and tell them to look it up in the dictionary. They usually thought I was kidding, after all words are not invented just like that, they just happen, but when they found it there they were impressed.

Unlike RUR there is nothing apocalyptic about "Gardener's Year." It is a gentle, humorous book about the joys and tribulations of gardening life. Capek wrote it after he built his house in Prague, and had to do something about the barren yard. The book is a series of short essays, one for each month of the year, plus a few extra ones. The "Gardener's Year" is still in print and I have a copy in English. Once in a while I dip into it to compare Uncle Karel's comments with my own gardening experiences.

Ever curious Uncle Karel wonders how a man becomes a gardener. "Odd as it may appear, a gardener does not grow from seed, shoot, bulb, rhizome, or cutting, but from experience, surroundings, and natural conditions. When I was a little boy I had towards my father's garden a rebellious and even vindictive attitude, because I was not allowed to tread on the beds and pick unripe fruit. Just the same way Adam was not allowed to tread on the beds and pick the fruit from the Tree of Knowledge in the Garden of Eden, because it was not yet ripe; but Adam - just like us children - picked the unripe fruit, and therefore was expelled from the Garden of Eden; since then the fruit of the Tree of Knowledge has always been unripe." By the way his father, Dr. Antonin Capek, was an enthusiastic gardener and hybridizer of roses. But, as far as I know, never wrote anything about it.

Starting the year Uncle Karel says: " In January the gardener cultivates the weather. There is something peculiar about the weather; it is never quite right. Weather always shoots over the mark on one side or the other." Then he goes on: "It would be quite nice if from the first of January it were nine-tenths of a degree below freezing, one hundred and twenty-seven millimeters of snow (light and, if possible, fresh), rather cloudy, calm, or with mild winds from the West; and all would be well.

But nobody minds us gardeners, and nobody asks us what things ought to be. That's why the world is as it is."

About garden work he decides: "If gardeners had been developing from the beginning of the world by natural selection they would have evolved most probably into some kind of invertebrate. After all, for what purpose has a gardener a back? Apparently only so that he can straighten it at times, and say: "My back aches!" As for legs, they may be folded in different ways; one may sit on the heels, kneel on the knees, bring the legs somehow underneath, or finally put them round one's neck..." Can anyone can disagree with that?

When he is talking about the art of gardening he says that, "..real gardener is not a man who cultivates flowers; he is a man who cultivates the soil. If he came into the Garden of Eden he would sniff excitedly and say: "Good Lord, what humus!""

Karel mentions he planted some birch trees with the thought there will be a grove of them, and a little seedling oak, but in the two years since it has grown little. Also there was the cedar of Lebanon, almost as big as he was, but that these cedars grow to a height of three hundred feet, and that he would love to see it mature - but "we must wait".

He concludes: "We gardeners live somehow for the future; if roses are in flower, we think that next year they will flower better, and in some few years this little spruce will become a tree - if only those few years were behind me! I should like to see what those birches will be like in fifty years. The right, the best is in front of us. Each successive year will add growth and beauty. Thank God that again we shall be one year farther on!"

He did not live long enough to see his trees mature, but I saw his garden fifty years later, and the birch grove was just as he imagined it. It gave me hope.

WAITING FOR SPRING

For gardeners there are only two seasons in the year - when they can work in the garden and when they cannot. The length of the two seasons depends on any number of factors, but the non-gardening season always appears longer.

The months between the last chrysanthemum and the first snowdrop are hollow and empty in a way that nothing except getting real dirt under one's nails can fill. Houseplants fall short. Seasonal festivities are just a feeble distraction. Imagination soars ahead to spring.

SHAKESPEARE'S PLANTS

January and February are the dark ages for gardening. It is usually too cold for neglected cleanup chores and much too early to start spring planting. The only comfort can be found in garden catalogs where it is always summer and no bugs or diseases mar the land.

But garden catalogs can be dangerous. Before you know it, you have ordered several dozen must-have plants for which you have no place in the garden, or money, when it shows up several months later on the credit card bill.

For that reason, I prefer to find solace in garden books. They don't seduce me to do something rash. Usually I just page through them for inspiration or look at the pictures, but recently I have been amusing myself with sort of trivia game, and amassing useless bits of knowledge. When I read something where an unfamiliar plant is mentioned, I try to find out about it.

Shakespeare is always very good for that. Take my favorite passage in Midsummer Night's Dream, where Oberon tells us where Titania, Queen of the Fairies, sleeps: "I know the bank where the wild thyme blows, Where oxlips and the nodding violet grows; Quite overcanopied with luscious woodbine, With sweet musk-roses and with eglantine."

I can cope with the wild thyme, although I don't see it blowing. As a rule, it grows only a few inches high. I have it in my herb garden right by the kitchen door. And yes, a large patch of it could make a fragrant bed. My herb encyclopedia speaks highly of Thymus vulagris, mentioning it was used to cure assorted psychological problems. A soup of beer and thyme was used to overcome shyness as well as nightmares. More to the point, it says that planting of thyme repels cabbage worms and whiteflies.

Oxlip is another matter. There is disagreement on what it exactly is. An annotated Midsummer Night's Dream pegs it a cross between cowslip and primrose. The garden book says it is the basic English primrose, Primula vulgaris, which is low and practically stalkless. The cowslip is another primula, a fragrant one, with yellow flowers carried on stalks. It is known as Primula veris.

Primulas of any shape, size or subgroup are nice to have in a garden. They are at their best in the spring when their bright colors dress up perennial beds. But they will sometimes also flower in the fall and into winter. I still have one hardy plant of the stalkless variety bravely showing its face.

Shakespeare's nodding violet is probably the sweet violet common to the colder parts of Europe. It looks much like our violet, but it has a fragrance which ours do not have. The flowers are, not surprisingly, violet color, although white varieties can be found.

When I lived in Europe, every spring bunches of them were sold on streets by urchins or others trying to make a bit of money on the side. The bunches were small, just large enough to pin as a corsage to a coat, and the sweet smell was pleasant. Young swains bought them for their sweethearts. It was an inexpensive way to make an impression.

What Shakespeare meant by woodbine is also uncertain. My various sources identify woodbine as a clematis, as a honeysuckle, or even as a Virginia creeper. The three of them are not identical, but all three of them are vines. That is all that matters in this case. Each could make a luscious canopy for Titania.

Musk rose is not what it sounds like. It is not a proper rose at all, but a musk mallow or Malva moschata, a type of hibiscus.

The European variety is a perennial which often grows alongside roads. The flowers are about two inches wide, white or rose colored, and they have a pleasant musklike scent. Our Rose of Sharon is a variety of a mallow, but it is not the "moschata". How well musk mallow would twine into the canopy I am not sure, but perhaps Shakespeare's variety was more of a vine.

Unlike musk rose, Eglantine is a real rose. It is usually called sweet briar. I would not care to sleep on it, but it makes a nice hedge, whether around Titania's resting place or in a garden. In early spring it can be closely clipped, and in summer it will produce pale pink blooms which mature into red rose hips. The foliage is fragrant, especially after rain.

It would be fun to plant a Shakespearean corner in the garden, but I am not sure it would do well. Our climate is different from the English one. To hot, too cold and not enough rain.

As Shakespeare wrote, "There sleeps Titania, sometime of the night, Lull'd in these flowers, with dance and delights." Perhaps the best thing is just dream about it.

THE ART OF HOUSE PLANT WATERING

Somewhere in the second month of winter I come to the conclusion that plants belong outside, and that it was a mistake to bring so many geraniums, petunias, begonias, impatients and other plants to over-winter in the house.

It is not that I don't enjoy them. The petunias, which were trimmed and replanted into hanging baskets are back with exuberant color, and the geraniums bloom better now than they did in the garden. But unlike outside, where the occasional rain took care of them, I am now their sole watering provider.

Let us admit it, watering inside the house is difficult.

First comes what to water when, so that some plants are not forgotten while others are flooded. This is a challenge with several dozen spread over window sills, tables and shelves throughout the house. Also different plants have different watering needs, from once a week to daily.

Then come the mechanics - how to deliver water where it is needed, without flooding the whole room. Or have water dripping like a Chinese water torture, on furniture or heads of people innocently minding their business.

I have not been able to solve the first problem - when to do it. That needs an organized person, with more time than I have, going around every day to look at each plant, lift it to feel how heavy it is (lighter pot means dry soil), and if in doubt stick a finger into the soil to feel for moisture. Instead of a finger there are commercial moisture meters to do the same thing. They work, but if they are left in the soil they will corrode and break down, which is not likely to happen with your finger.

The problem of water delivery has several solutions, but most important is to remember that deep and slow watering is best. Just because water runs through a pot does not mean the soil is moist. Very likely it is just the opposite.

One way is to have a good sized container of water, such as a wash tub or even the kitchen sink, submerge each plant in it, and wait a few minutes until bubbles of air stop coming up. Afterwards the flower pot needs to sit somewhere for the excess water drain out. I find this method messy because the loose soil floats and gets all over the kitchen sink.

My preferred watering system is by dripping. Since most of my faucets drip anyhow (this tends to happen in an old farmhouse), I make virtue from a fault. At any given moment I have a flower pot or basket sitting in the kitchen sink, or the bathroom washbasin, or the tub, getting slow drips of water. Occasionally I may rotate the pot so that all sides are affected although this is not necessary, the moisture will seep through all the soil eventually.

There are always some flower planters too large, or hanging inconveniently out of reach, and these are the hardest to water. Once in a while they should get deep watering, if at all possible - but there are alternatives. Soaking bottle works well, if the planter is large enough to hold it. Any plastic bottle with couple of holes punched in it and filled with water will drip away for hours. But do test you holes first in a sink to see how fast or slowly they work.

Another alternative is ice cubes. Yes, ice cubes. In a densely planted flower pot or basket, where no soaking bottle fits, there is always some spot for couple of ice cubes. And unless you dump the whole bucket on it they melt slowly enough for the water to sink in and not dribble out.

With the ice cubes I have been concerned whether they could damage tender plants. But this has not happened. I try to put the ice on the soil rather than on the plant itself, although often there is no other place to put it. But this does not seem to bother them.

Of course the absolutely best way to water house plants is to take them out into a nice rain. But, as I am writing this, it is 23F outside, so this is not now an option.

WINTER PLANTS

Recently, defying snow, ice and cold weather, I started looking around the garden to see what, if anything, was happening there. Well, it was not much, but it wasn't zero either.

I did not have to look far. Opening the kitchen door and looking down into the herb bed I saw a spot of bright yellow. At first I thought it was something chewed and left there by the dogs. But no. It was a plant, a flower, the first winter aconite had opened. As I rummaged under the drifts of leaves I found several more.

Winter aconites, properly known as Eranthis hyemalis, are the earliest to bloom. Garden catalogs list them as March blooming, but this was January, and it was way below freezing outside. They are compact plants, 2 to 4 inches high. The flowers are yellow and resemble buttercups - both in color and shape, and each blossom is cradled in a leaf collar of Toby dog's ruff.

I am always surprised by the aconites, and delighted. I am pleased that past summer's weeding and cultivating the bed had not destroyed them, that they came back. And I love their debonair attitude, blooming even if all around them is frozen or under snow.

I did not plant these aconites. I found them there. How long ago they were planted I am not sure, but I have been puzzled by one thing. According to all sources aconites naturalize easily, and will multiply vigorously. My two aconites have been in that spot over ten years and they have not produced any offspring. Well, not exactly. This year, finally, one of them has become a mother of three baby aconites.

Many garden catalogs carry aconites, usually in batches of 20 or more, because they do look best if they are massed. They should be planted about 2 inches deep in early fall, even in August if possible, so they develop vigorous roots before winter sets in. They prefer rich, moist soil and partial sun. The best place for them is in open ground, such as under trees or bushes. If they like their location they will live a long time - and multiply.

My other discovery was along the driveway. Several years ago I planted there winter jasmine, and true to its name it was cheerfully blooming. It looks much like its tender, scented cousin, but, alas, it has no fragrance. The small bell-like yellow flowers open sometimes as early as November on leafless branches. They will last through February.

Winter jasmine is often used as a climber (which it is) on a fence or wall, but it can be also used free standing as a bushy ground cover. I put it along the driveway because I wanted something that did not need mowing or watering and looked nice both summer and winter.

Winter jasmine spreads easily with long branches reaching in all directions and rooting if they come in contact with soil. This is an advantage if you are starting your planting. You can just get some cuttings and root them either in individual pots or directly where you want them to grow. They are easy to start, although they will need to be watered until they are well rooted and settled.

Some people cannot get jasmine to bloom. This happens when it is pruned too late in the season. The branches should be cut well back as soon as the blooms have faded, and not pruned again afterwards.

There is another plant which blooms in late winter - this is the winter sweet - Chimonanthus fragrans. Winter sweet is also a climber, best grown over a trellis against a wall. In January to February it has small, fluffy yellow flowers with reddish centers which are marvelously fragrant. These will turn by summer into nice looking brown pods.

Winter sweet is more of a southern plant. It is marginally hardy in our area, although if grown in a protected spot it can survive as far north as New York. The easiest way to propagate it is through layering the lower branches in spring. I have not seen the plants offered in any of the popular garden catalogs, but perhaps some that specialize in unusual shrubs may carry it.

In conclusion a passing thought. Why is it that most these winter blooming plants are yellow, or washed out pinks and soggy whites? Is winter just too harsh for bright colors like red, blue or purple?

LANGUAGE OF FLOWERS

If flowers could only talk, what tales would they tell. But of course they can, you just have to know the code.

Before the advent of e-mail and instant messaging there was the language of flowers, much appreciated by Victorian maidens and their swains. Posies were always given or exchanged. It was useful not only for communicating but also as a socially acceptable way to show attachment. The rule was that unmarried ladies could not accept presents of any value from men, except flowers or perhaps candy, but candy was already suspect.

I have an etiquette book called "Manners, Culture and Dress of the Best American Society" published in 1894, which devotes a full chapter to "Flowers and their Sentiments." It says, "Flowers are the smiles of nature, and earth would seem a desert without them. They grew first in Paradise, and bring to our view more vividly than anything else the beauties of Eden...." and more in the same vein.

Then it continues: "It is no new thing to attach sentiments to flowers. In eastern lands flowers have a language which all understand. It is that "still small voice" which is powerful on account of its silence. It is one of the chief amusements of the Greek girls to drop these symbols of their esteem or scorn upon the various passengers who pass their latticed windows."

"These customs have not been confined to the eastern countries alone, but have been taken up and to a large extent are recognized everywhere; and at the present time great care is taken in the cultivation of the flowers that express by their sentiments the subjects that are considered first among the young."

This is followed by a list of 325 possible statements accompanied by their floral equivalents. The list ranges from Age/Snow-ball tree to Zest/Lemon, and includes such items as Bond of love/Honeysuckle, Chaste love/Acacia, Constancy/Bluebell, Delicate beauty/Hibiscus, Slighted love/Yellow chrysanthemum, I am your captive/Peach blossom, and You occupy my thoughts/Violet.

But it also lists flowers for love scorned: Bluntness/Borage, Counterfeit/Mock orange, Drunkenness/Vine, I declare against you/Tansy, Fickleness/Lady's slipper, Rudeness/Clotbur, and Stupidity or Indiscretion/Almond tree.

I am not sure how it worked in practice. Dropping a blossom out of window to make a statement is one thing, but spelling out a message is another one - especially something poetic. It would depend on the message and the availability of the plants. Some sentiments might not be expressible at certain times of the year. Obviously substitutions had to be made and the young ladies were expected to fill in any blanks.

Luckily the Victorians had simple taste, such as it was, since that was an era of seriously bad taste. Their idea of poetry ran to something like: "Accept this message, Dearest I pray, From the one who loves you, 'tis Valentine's Day." The bouquet expressing that would include hawthorn for hope and a yellow tulip for declaration of love. There is no listing for 'message' or 'Valentine's Day' in my dictionary.

Even harder, if not impossible, would be to express Shakespeare's "O, Mistress mine, where are you roaming? O, stay and hear! your true love's coming." Although, of course, it is a much nicer poem.

I like the idea of flower language, despite its limitations, and if somebody sends me a sprig of yellow jasmine or a gillyflower or some other reddish pink, I would be thrilled. However, I would hate to get a bouquet of African violets. This would be saying that have a vulgar mind. Not true.

FORCING FLOWERS

If you shouldn't be spending your grocery money on fresh flowers for the house, but reach the point when looking at dried or silk flower arrangements makes you scream, and want to throw them out of the window, you are probably ready for forcing.

Relax, forcing is not some isometric exercise done with a crow bar slung over your back. It is a gentle art of persuading flowers to bloom before their time.

Great many plants can be forced. Certainly spring bulbs, but also spring flowering trees and shrubs. From mid-January on is a good time to do it, although with a very mild winter the plants can beat you to it. But if you try it earlier the buds don't get enough chilling to break dormancy, and the forcing will fail.

The most popular flowers for forcing are pussy willows and forsythias. These can be forced earliest because they have a short dormancy period. January is a good time for them. Flowering fruit trees can be forced as well. Just think about delicate apple or plum blossoms, or cherries, or almonds. The flowering quince, if you have one, is especially lovely because it has such interesting branches. Fruit trees do best when started in mid-February or even later.

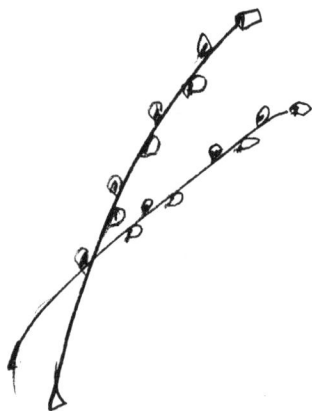

Other plants that can be forced are lilacs, witch hazels, hawthorns, mock oranges, spireas, wisterias and horse chestnuts. If you have other spring flowering trees or bushes that set their buds in the fall, you can experiment with them as well.

Choose the youngest branches with the largest buds and cut them about 2 to 3 feet long because this will look best in arrangements. The stems should be medium thickness or better, so they have enough stored sugars which are needed for nourishing the flower buds. Use sharp knife or pruning shears, cutting on the diagonal, just above a bud. After you bring the branches inside, strip the bottom few inches, removing any buds or small twigs. Then split or crush the ends with a hammer so that water can penetrate the stem.

At this point you can either arrange the bare branches and wait for them to flower, or plunge them into lukewarm water with floral preservative, store them in a cool spot, and wait for the buds to color and open. The buds will open within 2 - 6 weeks, depending on how close they are to their natural blooming time. The closer they are the faster they will open. You can control this, partly, by keeping them in a cooler room, to retard the blooming, or placing them on a sunny window to speed it up.

By cutting new branches every week, you can have fresh flowers from mid-winter till spring. But as you are cutting branches for forcing be careful where you cut. Think of it as pruning and consider how the tree or bush should look when you are finished with it.

To keep your arrangements longer, keep them out of direct sun, recut the stems every few days, and change the water in the container. And most of all enjoy them. These flowers will remind you that spring is just around the corner.

SPRING

T.S.Elliot was wrong. April is not the cruelest month, just the opposite. It is a month of hope, when anything and everything seems possible. Even if during a warm spell you have set out all your seedlings and a late frost got them. That does happen but it can be avoided, with some planning, such as covering them with flowerpots, or just-in-case saving some inside until later.

And besides there is always May, which makes up for it. By that time nature is in full bloom, all early mishaps are forgotten, and ahead is a whole new season of unlimited possibilities. You are confident that this year all will go well - a hope possible only in spring before the reality sets in.

SNOWDROPS

"The snow-drop, and then the violet,
Arose from the ground with warm rain wet..."

I wish I had thought of this myself, but it was written couple of hundred years ago by Shelley. And he put it down just right, this is how it happens - but few people notice, or care. Everyone tends to get excited by the eye-popping daffodils, or bright colored tulips you can see clear across the garden, while the small flowers that hug the ground get overlooked. They deserve better.

Snowdrops (Galanthus nivalis) are not showy but they are not shy either. They are perky, lighthearted, insouciant. They are not high maintenance plants - they give you a lot of pleasure with minimum work. Once you plant them they come up year after year, whether the weather is wet, dry, hot or cold. You don't have to worry about late frost or snow because they take it in their stride. You don't have to water them or fertilize them. Nothing seems to eat them, not even the deer - though I am not sure about rabbits.

Snowdrops will grow happily almost anywhere and look best in informal groups, under bushes or trees, along the edges of flower beds, or by a fence. After they get settled they multiply, eventually creating something like a soft white carpet. This may take a few years but you can hasten it if you transplant a few plants ahead of the main body and let those start spreading.

The blooms last several weeks, starting usually in February and ending some time in March. The best time to transplant them is after they finish blooming, but before their leaves die off for the summer - which they will eventually. After that they are pretty hard to find.

If you are starting from scratch the bulbs should be planted in late summer or fall. August is not too soon if you want early blooms. Most catalogs and garden shops carry snowdrop bulbs, and they are quite inexpensive. Plant the bulbs about three inches deep in good loam. If your soil is hard and clay, enrich it with leaf mold or compost, and add a bit of bulb fertilizer to the planting holes. And if the fall is dry watering them in helps. It gives the bulbs a good start on developing roots.

Come late winter the spiky leaves poke up, followed by the flower stems. The flowers will have 4" - 6" stems and can be cut and taken inside. I like them best plain in a small container with nothing but a bit of greenery, so they are not overwhelmed. But they can be combined with other small flowers that bloom early, such as the yellow winter aconites, purple grape hyacinths or blue scillas.

They would look well with the violets, but as Shelley said, violets usually come in later. In February violets are still curled up showing just the beginning of their leaves. The future flowers are in the center, stemless buds with barely a hint of color.

I don't know anyone who actually plants violets. Their fancier cousins, violas, yes, but violets just are. But they are not weeds, there is much to recommend them. With their purple blossoms they brighten the patio, punctuate garden walks, or edge the driveway. The leaves are pretty too and make a fine ground cover, except that they die down later in the season.

Violets can become pests left to their own devices. They reseed and start invading everything in the vicinity. But in spring they are most welcome. Over the years I have had a love-hate relationship with violets. I want them some places but not others - but they will not listen. So often I will dig large clumps of them from one area because they are impinging on some plants, and stick them elsewhere where is a void. Then couple of years later that spot gets overrun as well and we start all over again. Right now I am enjoying them, wherever they are, and when it rains I think about the old song: "It isn't raining rain to me, It's raining violets."

DAFFODILS

The cows are wading in daffodils - but not eating them as far as I can see - and the pasture is spotted with gold. Mama cows are watching their rambunctious calves which are running, hopping and flopping down in the daffodil patches.

The new calves are especially colorful this year. Besides the two basic black and white, there is one all black, and one pure white. The white calf is blindingly white, like a piece of paper, or a sheet of white plastic. I thought it was a piece of plastic the morning it was born, until I saw the ears sticking up. It is the cutest thing, and as frisky as the other three. Between the cows, calves and daffodils it is a lovely sight. The daffodils are all over the pasture. I am sure they were not planted there

on purpose, but over the past fifty or hundred years they were transported from the garden by restless moles, and they took root and multiplied.

The scene makes one think of Wordsworth's famous poem; "I wandered lonely as a cloud, That floats on high o'er vales and hills, When all at once I saw a crowd, A host, of golden daffodils," which crops up in school curriculums as faithfully as the flowers it celebrates. Unfortunately those flowers are not doing well. While my daffodils are going strong in Virginia, Wordsworth's English daffodils are disappearing. According a recent report they are in danger of extinction.

The culprit is not vandalism, pollution, or destruction of environment, but modern, hybrid daffodils. When Wordsworth wrote that poem in 1816, there probably were no hybrid daffodils. Or if there were, not within miles of this country meadow. But things have changed. Just as in my pasture, some cultivated, garden daffodils have drifted into the fields, the bees and bugs did their bit with cross pollinating, and now the small, dainty wild daffodils are becoming less so. Their stems are getting longer and the blooms larger. As it often happens to native plants a vigorous intruder overwhelmed them.

Until I read it in the paper, I never thought about daffodils being subject to cross pollination as they are propagated by bulb division not seeds. But they do develop seed pods, and these can be planted. Eventually the seeds will grow into a new plant. But to bloom it takes five or more years from the time of sowing and is no sure thing. It only makes sense when developing new varieties, on purpose, or accidentally as in Wordsworth's meadow.

English people tend to take their gardening seriously, and their literature as well, so this is for them an alarming situation. But short of digging out all the interlopers, and then putting up a high wall or a dome over the pasture, so no stray pollen can get in, there probably is nothing anyone can do. The big new hybrids will substitute for the native ones. And some people may even like them better.

This matter of substitution reminded me of another article, very much apropos Wordsworth's poem on daffodils. I found it in a recent issue of Atlantic magazine. It was written by Phyllis Rose, who likes daffodils but is no fan or Wordsworth.

Ms Rose wrote about people who, as a game, perk up various ossified verses. You could call it a literary parody, but they call it N plus 7. It consists of substituting another noun chosen from a dictionary, for each noun in a poem. Ideally it should be the seventh noun found in the dictionary following the original one, however if the seventh noun does not fit the rhyme or meter, one can go on until it does. As you can imagine this produces splendidly surreal effects, much like looking at an object through a distorted lens or mirror. But the poetry remains. The

Wordsworth poem is a fine example.

Rose quotes several versions of the poem, using different dictionaries - which can change it dramatically, and produce text ranging from
dull nonsense to sublime chaos. The punchiest transformation was put
together by Harry Matthews, using a standard English-German dictionary. The text reads:

> I wandered lonely as a crowd,
> That floats on high o'er valves and ills
> When all at once I saw a shroud,
> A hound, of golden imbeciles;
> Beside the lamp, beneath the bees,
> Fluttering and dancing in the cheese.

There are two more stanzas to the poem and then it concludes:

> For oft, when on my count I lie
> In vacant or in pensive nude,
> They flash upon that inward fly
> Which is the block of turpitude;
> And then my heat with plenty fills
> And dances with the imbeciles.

Isn't this wonderful? You are welcome to check it against the
original, if you wish, to see which is better, but I, ignoring the block of
turpitude, shall join the golden imbeciles and pensively flutter and dance
in the cheese.

JOHNNY - JUMP - UP

He is a nimble, enterprising fellow. Brings to mind a cute guy,
maybe eight, ten years old, who can't sit still, gets into all sorts of trouble
- but is fun to have around. This is Johnny-jump-up, the wild pansy, or
Heartsease, or if you want to use the proper botanical name, Viola tricol-
or. Under any name it is the ancestor of our cultivated pansies.

Johnny-jump-up is the pansy of Shakespeare's time. When he had

Ophelia speak of rosemary for remembrance, the same sentence conclud-
ed: "and there is pansies, that's for thought." Why for thought I am not
sure, but those little flowers spark imagination. Another name for them
was Love-in-idleness, and an early English writer described them: "By
reason of the beauty and braverie of their colors, they are very pleasing to
the eye, for smell, they have little or none."

And pleasing to the eye they are for most of the year. They appear
among the first flowers of spring. This year they were popping up from
between the bricks in the walk even before the crocuses opened. And
despite the vagaries of weather, going from cold to hot and from dry to
wet and dry again, they are still there, still blooming. They don't ask for
any special care, no watering, fertilizing or pruning is required.

These little pansies return year after year, but they are not perennials. The mature plants die eventually, but they self seed, so next year
there is another crop, spread even wider, and so to eternity.

Johnny-jump-ups can be started from seed, and in spring some
nurseries also carry the plants as seedlings. Or you can ask for a plug or
two from a friend who has them. If seeded, an early start is best, perhaps
inside, and then transplanted outside before the weather gets hot. If they
are left in place you will not have to worry about next year's crop.

I don't have a neat garden so I don't find them invasive. I rather
enjoy the small sparks of color mixed in with other plants. But some people, neater than I, may want to limit the Johnny-jump-ups from spreading. The best way is to pull out the plants as they start setting seed, which
takes close observation, and some seeds will always come through. The
next step is to pull the little seedlings as they appear in late winter or
early spring.

If the common Johnny-jump-up does not tempt you there are
many other cultivated violas, some of them even fragrant. By the way
violas are smaller and hardier versions of pansies, and should be treated
the same.

But I am perfectly happy with my plain vanilla Johnny-jump-up,
with the purple petals and white and yellow centers, plus those that are
purple and lilac or where a little bit of white creeps in. They are light-

hearted, amusing, and I can depend on them.

TULIPS

Last Christmas I got a book with the subtitle "The Story of a Flower That Has Made Men Mad." It could have been called "The Story of a Flower That Made Men Act Like Fools." It was about tulips, of course.

Tulips do strange things to people. Everyone knows about the Dutch "Tulipomania" which made today's stock market appear anemic in comparison. In 1623 a tulip bulb called "Semper Augustus" went for 1,000 florins, when the average annual income was about 150 florins. The tulip was described as white with carmine on a blue base and an unbroken flame right to the top. That was the beginning. Each year the price rose, to 5,000 florins in 1633, and finally in 1638 to 13,000 florins for a single bulb. That was more than the cost of a most expensive mansion in the center of Amsterdam.

Today we don't get so carried away, but tulips can still bring on a touch of madness. Caught in a spell of full color catalog we order a dozen varieties with 10 or more bulbs each, even though the only place to put them is the driveway, or plow under the front lawn. And if you choose the rarer varieties, the cost can add up.

Spring is the time to start thinking about next year's tulips. Old ones - that you want to bloom again - and new ones to be planted in the fall. As you see them - their location, their colors - you can visualize what you want or do not want next year. This is why bulb growers start bombarding us with their catalogs before the tulip blooms have faded.

It helps to remember that tulips are not perennials. They are annuals where the bulb disintegrates after it blooms, forming a daughter bulb in its place. (Crocus and gladioli work the same way.) With proper care and feeding the bulbs can be encouraged to come back and bloom year after year.

The three most important steps in perennializing tulips are the right variety of a tulip suited to the local climate, a well-drained planting bed and fertilizing. The fine print in bulb catalogs, or on the small labels of tulip packets, will say whether the tulip is early, mid or late blooming, but also whether it is suitable for naturalization. Buy the so-called perennial or naturalizing bulbs if you want to keep them. And then plant your tulips deep enough. Shallowly planted bulbs will bloom well the first year, but in the following years they will get smaller blooms with shorter stems until they disappear. About six inches is the right planting depth, though in sandy soil it can be even more.

The biggest need in fertilizer is for nitrogen. The bulbs should get their first feeding when they are planted, and be fed again in spring when the foliage emerges. Bone meal used to be the first choice for bulbs, but it may have more phosphorus and less nitrogen. Fertilizer such as 10-10-10 or 8-8-8 is preferable. Besides, with bone meal, dogs think there is a bone buried there and dig up all your lovingly planted bulbs.

The breath-taking tulip displays you see in public parks or gardens use tulips as annuals. Often this makes sense. Once the blooms fade, even if you deadhead them, the foliage starts drooping, yellowing, and you are left with a flower bed of mangy looking leaves. You can either dig the bulbs up and throw them away, or try to hide the old foliage with annuals. But do not cut it away, or tie it in knots, if you want the tulips to bloom next spring.

My own preference is for the flamboyant, multicolored Rembrandt and parrot tulips, so beloved to the old Dutchmen. Alas, they have not thrived in my garden. At best they last a year - that is if the bulbs are not eaten by the voles. But I have a number of totally wild red tulips which pop up every few years in the most unexpected places - such as in the middle of the lawn. In off years they display just one lonely leaf. I don't know where they were originally planted, or when. But there they are, again and again.

MAGNOLIAS

"Magnolias will break your heart," an old gardening friend told me many years ago as we were looking at my little blooming tree, "you do not want to plant them here." But because for some perverse reason I always fall in love with the most unsuitable object I can find, I have now half a dozen magnolias in my garden. Yes, they break my heart, but I love them passionately.

What can be more enchanting than a magnolia blossom? The large cup-like flowers crimson on the outside, but shell pink inside, hint at magic. Or they can be all white with just a tinge of pink, or yellow.

The downside is that magnolias are impetuous. Instead of biding their time for dependably frost free nights, they decide to bloom at the first warm spell of spring. Then, after a day or few, there is another frost. Magnolia blossoms, and even buds, are very sensitive to frost. Next morning the spectacular flower laden tree is a sad looking object covered with withered, ugly brown globs. This is heartbreaking. The globs stay there until weeks later the leaves open and hide them.

There are some 80 species of magnolias. Some are evergreen and bloom in summer, others are deciduous, losing their leaves in winter and blooming in spring. Most magnolias came from Asia, but some originated in North America - even in Virginia. The first specimen to arrive in Europe, in 1688, was called Magnolia virginiana. This is also known as sweet bay or swamp laurel. By the way, magnolias got their name from Pierre Magnol (1638-1715) who was a director of botanic garden at Montpellier in France. Why he was so honored my sources do not say.

Although some of the varieties are not winter hardy, most are. Magnolias can be grown as far north as Canada. Best are the hybrids, such as the soulangiana varieties or the star (stellata) magnolias. The soulangianas will grow big, eventually very big. For small gardens, star magnolias are a wiser choice. Instead of reaching 30 feet or more, they stop at 12 to 15 feet. They can be pruned if necessary. This should be done during the summer before next year's buds form. Removing smaller branches will not harm a young tree, but cutting off large branches, especially from older trees, is not recommended.

Magnolias should be planted in spring, while they are in bud or starting to bloom, but still leafless. They like a sunny location, but preferably not southern exposure, which speeds up bud break. Once they are settled they do not need much care. Other than their habit of blooming too early, magnolias are trouble free. Their requirements are simple; fairly good, well-drained soil, and if possible a little peat or compost placed about the roots at planting time. They do not like lime soil however.

Most magnolias will bloom young. If you buy your tree from a catalog you may get a slender twig, which could surprise you next spring with a blossom or two. These blossoms are announced by pussy willow-like buds that appear at the end of the twigs. Unfortunately, the silvery buds are tempting to small children and dogs. Because they are so soft and pretty they will happily pry them off, unless you stop them. By the time the tree gets big this is no longer a problem.

With magnolias, some years you win, some years you lose. So if you are either a gambler or philosophically inclined do include a magnolia in your garden. What can you lose but your hope? And that, as we know, always rises again -- like next year.

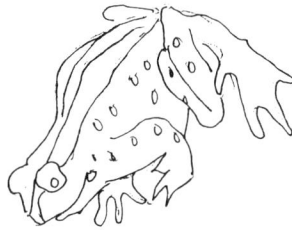

MAY IN THE GARDEN

Happiness is when our hopes and expectations are met, and life is such that they seldom are. Which is what makes happiness precious rather than dull. But things can get still worse. The desired can not only disappoint us but hurt us as well.

As the princess meets the frog, gives in to his entreaties, kisses him, he remains an ugly frog. Common enough. There are many more frogs than princes in the ponds of life. But if she comes down with major case of hives, because she is allergic to him, that is unfair. Even if he doesn't remain a frog.

Such things can happen in the garden. Especially in the month of May. After the bleakness of winter we are being seduced by nature to start planting things. The air is shining, the sun is warm, and all around us things are growing and blooming --- and releasing pollen. Wham! The nose starts running, the eyes gum up shut. If you are a gardener you cannot give in. There is no escaping into hermetically air-conditioned rooms and enjoying the garden through double glazed windows. What you do is try to ignore the symptoms, or take a few pills, and soldier on.

Any discomfort is offset by the happy surprises that every spring brings - the forget-me-not that survived and is blooming, azaleas which looked dead a month ago now in full color, a clematis coming up with white blossoms as big as saucers, and all the bright red oriental poppies popping up in the most improbable places. And they all want attention - weeding, pruning, fertilizing, as they promise marvelous rewards. The garden is like the frog. The magic kiss is the care which turns it into a prince. This cannot wait, it must be done now - or usually last week.

Pollens come and pollens go. After some rain they will settle down. As you are standing there, wiping your nose on a grubby gardening glove, you look around at all the color - your visions of spring have been met, and you feel just fine.

And for the sake of long term happiness, it helps if there are also some disappointments - such as the bleeding heart which has disappeared. New research shows that people tend to feel unsatisfied when they have everything, be it a kid on Christmas morning or a dot.com millionaire after a big kill. They ask: "Is that all there is?" There is now even a book with that title. I have not read it, and shall not read it. Not enough time, I have work to do in the garden. Obviously the answer is: No, of course not. But some of it should be also bitter. That sweetens the rest.

LILACS

I wonder what Walt Whitman really had on mind, when he wrote: "When lilacs last in the door yard bloom'd - And the great star early droop'd in the western sky in the night - I mourn'd and yet shall mourn with ever-returning spring." Had his lilacs died, or had an off year?

These things happen. Lilacs are hardy, dependable, but they can be temperamental too. After years of fragrant blossoms they suddenly stop blooming or come up with just a few scrawny specimens.

Several things can cause this. Most likely the bush has become overgrown, crowded, and needs thinning. To fix this cut out close to the ground all old and dead branches, as well as some branches in the center of the plant to let light in. The other possibility is that there are too many suckers, those little shoots which spring up from the ground around it.

Remove them. You can pot them or plant them elsewhere, and unless they come from grafted stock, they will grow into new bushes identical to the parent. It is also possible that the bush is not getting enough sunshine. Perhaps a new house was built in the vicinity or other trees are shading it. Lilacs need sun to bloom. There is no substitute for that.

Sometimes if buds are formed but fail to open, the culprit is drought the fall before when the buds were set. Nothing can be done about that, except replace moisture in the ground and wait for next year. Actually lilacs are fairly drought resistant, but some years may be too dry even for them.

If the new leaves turn brown this can also be a sign of drought, or something else. Such as transplanting injury or too much fertilizer. Often lilacs develop gray mildew on the leaves. This happens in late summer or fall. Although unsightly it does not harm the bush, but it is a good idea to rake up the mildewed leaves and get them out of the way, into garbage or burn them.

What encourages blooming is deadheading. As the blooms die remove them. This should be done when the old blossoms get brown and start forming seeds. But, if you cannot get to it, do not despair. Your lilacs will bloom next year, even if not quite so fully.

When planting lilacs, select good, well drained soil, not too acid. Lilacs like it alkaline. They will be happy alongside walls or house foundations where some lime leaches out, or every other year give them a bit of lime or wood ashes. Otherwise they should not be fertilized or they would grow too tall. Lilacs can be planted either in spring or fall, or almost any other time when the ground is not frozen solid.

If you have old lilacs that have grown too tall, or need to be rejuvenated, the best time to prune them is just after blooming. Most lilacs if left unpruned will grow to 10 to 20 feet, depending on variety, and the Japanese lilac could reach 40 feet. Lilac will tolerate drastic pruning, practically to the ground, but best is to about two to three feet. It will come back. But it will take couple of years for it to bloom again. If you want to have blooms every year prune only one third of unwanted branches, followed next year by the second one third, and finish it the third year.

Although some sources say that all lilac came to Europe from Persia in the 16th century, this is doubtful. Some lilacs are probably native to Hungary or borders of Moldavia. In the 1597 Herbal there is a description of something called "blue pipe privet" which is undoubtedly lilac as we know it. This lilac was carried by the European settlers to America and can still be found growing in old gardens. There are at least 25 other species of lilacs, originating in Asia and Europe. The French lilacs are called so because they were hybridized in France. The Latin name of lilac is Syringa, which tends to be confusing because by Syringas we usually mean mock orange.

One of the reasons for growing lilacs is their fragrance. But one can have too much of a good thing. The natural lilac scent is wonderful, but the lilac scent found in perfumes is too cloying. Somewhere I read that Colette described the lilac scent as "the discreet smell of scarab beetles." I don't know how scarab beetles smell, but I have been curious about it ever since.

FORGET- ME- NOTS

Forget-me-not, forget-me-not, forget-me-not, what a lovely, evocative name for such a modest little flower. It makes you think of poetry and wonder how it got its name, and yearn for things which never were. Its proper, scientific name is Myosotis, which is derived from the Greek 'mys' - mouse, and 'otos' - the ear. To put it bluntly it is called a 'mouse's ear'. But let's ignore that. It just spoils the mood.

Forget-me-nots appear as green mounds which in spring are covered with hundreds of small flowers on 6 to 12 inch stems. The flowers are no more than 1/4 inch across but they are many of them, and from distance they look like a delicate drift of color. They blend well with tulips, or candytuft, or columbines, and last about a month. Then they go to seed and die out. As they are dying off they tend to get leggy and flop over. However, it is a bad idea to clear them out at this point, as I did, unless you do not want them to come back next year. They need this time to reseed themselves. Small seedlings appear in fall, which will bloom the following spring.

We think of forget-me-nots as always being blue. Not so. Sometimes they are white or even pink. They like shady, moist places, but in boggy areas they will tolerate full sun. There are two kinds of forget-me-nots, biennial and perennial. The perennial variety is usually found alongside ponds. They do not blossom as profusely as their biennial cousins, but will flower over a longer season, from spring through summer.

The easiest way to start forget-me-nots is by seeding them in the ground where you want them to grow. Late summer is the best time. This lets them settle down before winter. They can be also started indoors in early spring and when large enough transplanted into the garden. These may or may not bloom that year. If they do not they will overwinter and bloom the following spring.

According to an old German tradition the name came from the last words of a knight who was drowned as he was trying to get the flower for his lady love. Perhaps. Or perhaps not. The poets made forget-me-nots a symbol of constancy, but they were probably not gardeners. For me constancy is something like petunias which start blooming in May and keep at it till the big frost kills them. And if you take them inside they will bloom through most of the winter. But forget-me-nots tease you. They bloom passionately in spring, disappear by summer, and may reappear as seedlings in different spots later.

There is something mercurial and ambivalent about them, as if they dared you both to remember and forget them. Just like some people? As the poet wrote: "I remember the way we parted, the day and the way we met; You hoped we were both broken-hearted, and knew we should both forget."

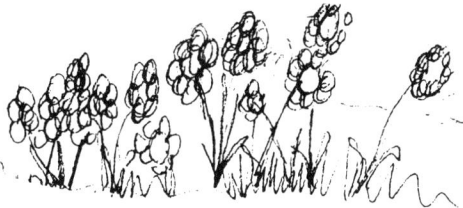

THE MAGIC CARPET

The old balladeer said. "There are twelve months in all the year, But the merriest month in all the year, Is the merry month of May." Indeed. May is a glorious month in the garden. Everything tries to bloom at the same time. Even the green stuff is greener somehow, much brighter and fresher. No wonder that songs and poems sing May's praise.

My garden which evolves into a wild jungle by summer, or a desert if there is drought, is now romantic. It is filled with pale blue bearded iris, cheerful daisies mixed with all sorts of columbines, oriental poppies, and now the peonies are opening, and they are spectacular. Especially the old one by the smokehouse cabin. It is a single petal white peony with a yellow center, and this year the blossoms are the size of dinner plates. How long it has been there I don't know. The smokehouse was built in the early part of the 19th century.

I am enjoying it all, spending much time just looking at the flow-ers instead of weeding. But, the last couple of days I kept finding excus-es to walk up the hill to look at the driveway. No, I am not mad, there is a reason.

Usually there is nothing special about my driveway. It winds its way up the hill, goes through the gate, and then turns around a tree near the side of the house. It is covered with gravel which bleeds into the surrounding grass. It is never going to appear in Garden Design or Architectural Digest. It is a perfectly average driveway, lacking charm, except in May. To be specific just a few days in May, when both the big buckeye and the holly trees are blooming.

The buckeye anchors the driveway which circles it. It is a mature tree, now more than hundred feet tall and bushy. Its crown covers the whole turnaround and then some. Come first week of May the flower candles open. Unlike other buckeyes, or common horse chestnuts, the flowers are not white but a deep shade of pink. The centers are yellow. It is a majestic sight, especially early in the morning when the sun hits it - although it is not at all bad in moonlight either. After about a week the individual blossoms start dropping, usually on my car, but on the ground too. And before long the top of the driveway looks like a pink shag carpet.

The holly tree sits next to the buckeye outside the driveway loop and it is pretty big too. It is no fancy kind, just your regular indigenous holly. It blooms also in May, which is fortunate. A note about holly trees. There are male trees and female trees, and as one would expect you need both to get berries, and then down the line new baby hollies. The one by the driveway is a male. Of course it blooms, but it does not have berries. The blossoms are small delicate things. They are white, have four petals and are no more than quarter of an inch across. They grow in clusters, and they are fragrant. Soon they start dropping their petals as well.

That is when the miracle happens. The tiny white petals fall on top of the pink buckeye blossoms and the ground turns almost iridescent. It becomes a shimmering carpet of pink with a touch of yellow and dots of white which look like loose pearls. This wonder lasts only a day or two, but it brings your pulse up every time you look at it. It makes you want to sit there, run your fingers through the soft petals and drink it all in.

I am a sucker for beauty. An old Alan Jay Lerner song drifts out of memory, "...once there was a spot, for one brief shining moment, that was known as Camelot." This is it. The weeding can wait.

SUMMER

If spring is about romance then summer is about passion - sometimes misguided. Things start getting out of bounds. The innocent sprigs of greenery grow into monstrous weeds which laugh to your face and defy you to destroy them. Bugs, beetles and caterpillars invade your garden with military precision, knowing exactly where to attack first, second and last.

But there are compensations. The vegetable patch is in full production so you can share your bounty with all the critters. And there are flowers giving color to the garden and still more for the house.

And, if things get really out of hand, this is the time to sit on the porch or front stoop and give in to the lazy feeling. Summer is also a fine time for rest.

PETUNIAS

There are some gardeners, who grow only perennials. They tend to call themselves 'plantsmen', but they plant no annuals in their gardens. Whatever their reasons, and there must be more than one, they find perennials more interesting. Perhaps they are. But this also suggests that to them perennials are worthier, more refined, while annuals are somehow vulgar, or, at best, a cliché.

I don't quite get this. I like annuals. They may be brash, and a bit pushy with their colors. But so what, I like their vitality. And perhaps coincidentally I often enjoy clichés as well. A good cliché packs a wallop, which is why it became popular in the first place.

Think about having as much fun as a barrel of monkeys, or someone dumb enough to fall off the turnip truck. The first person who thought of it had imagination, even though the logic is a bit shaky. Monkeys in a barrel could feel uncomfortable, and it is no dumber to fall off a turnip truck than off a potato truck. But expressions like these have color - a lot of it.

Which brings me to one of the most colorful and uninhibited annuals - the petunias. They are the mainstay of flower boxes where they cascade exuberantly, they fill in all sorts of otherwise barren flower beds, and they bloom from spring until frost, and beyond, if you take them inside.

There are delicately colored petunias, light pinks and whites and lavenders, but some of the best are the brights ones, the reds, and purples, the striped ones and the bright blues. Many of them are even fragrant.

I fell in love with petunias in Maine, where summers are short and intense. With frosts lasting deep into spring and starting again in early fall, you want something vigorous and bright, something that will take the summer heat but adjust to cooler nights of the fall. And something that will bloom and bloom.

It used to be that one had to deadhead fading blossoms or the plant would go to seed. The new varieties are much easier. They go on blooming even while forming a string of seed pods. But they will perform better if they are cut down in mid-summer, or whenever they get too straggly. Pruning a few of the stems at a time, over a period of several weeks, leaves you with enough blossoms to hide the cuts. As you do this give them a stiff dose of fertilizer and they will reward you with a new growth.

The easiest way to get your petunias is as plants in flats. The local nurseries have many kinds and colors and the seedlings transplant easily. But during hot or dry weather it is important to transplant them in the late afternoon, or when it is overcast, into a well watered soil, and then cover them with a basket or a flowerpot for couple of days, until they get settled. And of course they should not be allowed to dry out, although once they are established they tolerate drought well enough.

It is possible to start petunias from seed. The seeds germinate easily, but it takes a long time for them to get to the transplanting stage. I start mine in early March, at the latest, and even then the first blossoms do not show up until June.

As I was looking through some of my notes on petunias I saw that "Petun" means 'tobacco' in one South American Indian dialect, and that their leaves are supposed to have a similar narcotic effect as tobacco on humans. I am not sure how this works, and if this holds true for our hybrid varieties, or if it is true only for the original petunias. My source did not offer any details. And having given up tobacco years ago I certainly did not try smoking them.

The original petunias came in three species: P.axillaris, violacea and integrifolia, and they were short lived perennials. Their single trumpet flowers were much smaller than our petunias and certainly never ruffled. The colors were limited to white, pink or violet. Today you will get similar flowers if you let your hybrid petunias reseed themselves couple of years. They will return but the flowers will be smaller and the colors washed out.

As I write this, it looks like we may have a hot, dry summer. In that case make the best of it and plant flowers that can take it. Get some petunias, and have as much fun with them as a barrel of monkeys.

CLEOME

I once had an evening dress of silk chiffon in a color drifting from the lightest egg shell rose to deep pink. It was bias cut and layered and it felt like wearing a sunrise tinted cloud. I loved it. That dress still may be in one of the boxes in the attic, but even if I could get into it, which is doubtful, there is no place to wear it. Where to? - Kroger? - Wal-Mart? But I am always reminded of it when my cleomes are blooming, because they look just like that dress.

Cleomes are elegant, regal looking flowers. They can reach five to six feet. The leaves are star shaped, on sturdy stems which require no staking, ending with spectacular flower clusters. For some strange reason cleomes are also known as spider flowers. I cannot see any resemblance, and as far as I know spiders don't care about them one way or another. But butterflies and hummingbirds love them.

The wonderful thing about cleomes is that they start blooming young, and keep on blooming without need for dead-heading. They just get taller. Those ethereal balls of color refuse to turn brown and ugly. They keep on regenerating themselves, starting in the center with small buds, these grow larger, open, bloom, and go to seed, but the process continues on and on.

As the individual flowerlettes open and mature they change color, from almost white buds to vivid pink, the exact shades of my old dress. But gardeners who are not into pink can grow cleomes too. There are white, lilac and crimson varieties. Later each flowerette becomes a slender seed pod. These stick out from the stem like whiskers on a cat, while the top goes on blooming. By fall there is this tall, sticky stalk with pods surrounding the stem, but on the top new blooms continue to open.

Cleomes are native to South and Central America. They are annuals, and they reseed themselves easily. Left to their own devices, plus wind and meandering animals, the seeds will find their way to all corners of the garden.

Last year a few cleomes appeared in flower boxes on the terrace. They drifted there from back of the carriage barn where they had been planted a couple of years earlier. I did not remove them until spring. Of course, this year there is a whole bunch of cleomes growing in the walk below the terrace. They seem happy in the cracks of the bricks, and bloom too, even if they never get watered. But given the spartan environment they are only couple of feet tall. Perhaps in due time they will catch up with the others.

Since cleomes were originally tropical plants it takes them a while to get going. They do best if seeded inside and then transplanted out in mid-spring. Once the weather gets warm they develop quickly, and the plants start blooming while still small.

The self seeded plants take their time too. The seedlings just hang about until it gets warm, and then grow in a hurry. Cleomes do not mind slightly boggy soil, but in my garden they never get it, more likely the opposite. When they feel dry, they are champion droopers, wilting dramatically, but a timely watering brings them back.

In flower arranging cleomes present a challenge. Their stems are sticky, and they do not bend, standing there like a maypole. So care has to be taken when combining them with other flowers. I like them best plain, just two three stems in a tall glass vase.

Unlike most flowers which are best while young and fresh, cleomes stay interesting as they mature, after their seed pods form. The long stems become covered by small leaves and from it project slender stalks with the seed pods at the end. This makes a graceful support for the still blooming flowers. The combination is dignified and lighthearted at the same time, and achingly lovely.

I wish I could go to seed as gracefully as cleomes. But lets be realistic, that is rare even among the flora, and pretty much unattainable for the human race.

NIGELLA

If one Nigella is lovely, and three or four are great, the sight of thousands of them is awesome - especially when they are all going to seed. There is no doubt that something must be done - immediately - or next year's garden will have Nigellas from fence to fence, and from the front door to the rear, covering all, including the wood pile and perhaps even the cars. I am not joking. Some time ago I saw a Nigella seedling sprouting in some dirt in a corner of the pickup truck.

Nigellas are annuals and they self seed themselves vigorously. They look somewhat like bachelor buttons and come in colors from deep purple, through shades of blue, pale pink and white. There is even one yellow variety. The blossoms are about one and one-half inches across, with pointed petals floating above a collar of green lacy leaves. This probably is why they are called Love-in-a-mist.

Nigellas make good cut flowers. Because of their lacy foliage they are easy to arrange and they keep well. Even if some of the flower petals start to fall, the seed pods look graceful. And these pods, when dried, are wonderful in winter arrangements.

The best way to grow Nigella is from seed, preferably seeding them where they will stay. They like sunny locations but are not picky about the soil. This can be done very early in spring because the seedlings seem impervious to cold. My self-seeding plants show up already during winter, any time it is not brutally cold, and manage to survive to bloom in April and May.

This hardiness makes Nigellas ideal for planting in bulb beds. They come up just in time for hiding daffodil or tulip foliage when it flops over and looks like a start for a compost pile. If you want a longer period of bloom, you can start the seeds in several two-week intervals. When seedlings get a few inches high, they should be thinned to six to eight inches apart. But they don't mind being a bit crowded; crowding produces upright stems.

Most of the seed catalogs list several varieties of Nigellas. You can also ask for seeds from friends, or you may find them on some of the dried arrangements at plant sales and fairs.   In any case once you start growing Nigellas you'll never be without them - whether you want to or not.

FRAGRANCE

Fragrance of flowers is divine, but these days it gets lost in the shuffle. In a rush to get more colorful or bigger flowers scent counts for less and less. We go for the obvious, ignoring the subtle.

But it does not make sense. When you think of the old fashioned flowers, fragrance was always part of it. It was the heady smell of lilacs wafting through a window that meant spring. I have old lilacs which smell that way, while the new fancy ones do not.

Peonies too had their unmistakable scent. A whiff of it brings back memories. The best peonies bloomed in June, just in time for the Corpus Cristi celebration, so their petals could be scattered on the ground for the church procession to walk on. And I have always loved the spicy aroma of carnations. But I have not seen - I mean smelled - any like that for ages.

The old roses had a short blooming season, just a few weeks, but they had hundreds of blossoms, and their fragrance defined summer. I once picked up a mangled yellow climber on a Maryland roadside, as highway crews were bulldozing it for a new highway. After planting it by the house, where it soon covered the whole wall, the rose had each spring hundreds of buttery yellow flowers, with a subtle, spicy smell. I cherished it even though the flowers lasted only a day inside, and the bush bloomed less than a month.

That we tend to ignore fragrance in plants is puzzling, because otherwise we are fixated on it. Is it that we prefer the artificial to the real? If you look at the shelves of supermarkets, or in drugstores, scents are big, very big. There is no corner of our houses, or part of our bodies, which does not have several products designed to make them smell different.

The kitchen should not smell like a kitchen, whatever that may mean, but should smell like cinnamon or apple pie. The bathroom should smell like a lemon, or perhaps if you are the outdoor type like a pine. As far as the other rooms go you have choices; vanilla, peach, or strawberry for the dining room, something called spring meadow in the living room, and for the bedroom be romantic and make it lavender. But unfortunately all this is fake, and none of it smells like the real stuff.

When it comes to our bodies things get even worse, and the scents stronger. Every shampoo, cream, lotion or soap is lavishly perfumed so when you finish your toilette all the scents proceed to fight it out. No wonder that our sense of smell is overwhelmed - and deteriorating.

To me how things smell is important, but I don't like to be clobbered by it. Whether it is inside or out. Most flowers are not aggressively fragrant, although some are. For instance tuberoses. I like them, but only outside; inside they are overpowering.

It is the same with perfumes. They should never walk first into the room or hang around after the person leaves. Unfortunately most American perfumes will do this if applied generously. With a bit of practice you can come into a room and identify Armani here, Estee Lauder there, and in the corner Giorgio or a Calvin Klein. French perfumes are not so public. They are intimate.

A classic example of olfactory torture is sitting in a movie behind two people with incompatible perfumes, and the air-conditioning blowing it in your direction. Lately I have been suffering when paging through some of the big glossy magazines which have perfume flaps every twenty pages. After a couple of hundred pages it all smells the same - and so do you. When you finish you need to have a shower or at least thoroughly wash your hands.

My own favorite perfume, the one I have used most of my life, is Chanel's Russian Leather, which has not been sold in this country for over twenty years. This was a problem. But few years ago I read that they were beginning to import it again, so I asked around if anyone had it. No luck. Finally, when I was in New York, I ventured into the Chanel boutique in Rockefeller Center. That was an experience.

At the door I was greeted by a impeccably tailored young man who asked what was I looking for. I timidly said that I was wondering if they had my Russian Leather, because I have been unable to get it any-where else. The young man, looking at my country bumpkin persona, narrowed his eyes, pursed his lips, and in a clipped accent replied: " But, madame, of course we have it. We've have always had it, .." and then dripping with scorn added, " but you won't find it in places like depart-ment stores."

They did have it and I bought it. On the way out, as the young man was opening the door for me again, I firmly resisted remarking that living in the country we did not do much shopping in department stores. But that at the Farmer's Coop I can buy myself cow udder balm for my hands, and every year a brand new pair of overalls.

BLACK EYED SUSAN

"Ochi czorne, ochi vyorne," goes a Russian song, a favorite of sentimental late night song fests of my youth. It means; "Dark eyes (actually black eyes), are faithful eyes."

This song perfectly describes the patches of black-eyed-Susans growing in various corners of my garden. I like them there, but I am not sure I should. Between thinking what to do with the plants, if anything, I also wonder what the song really means.

Sure, one meaning is obvious - dark-eyed sweethearts are constant. And by implication blue-eyed people are fickle - but in a Russian song? A true Russian is always blue-eyed. Brown-eyed are the Tartars, the Gypsies and other wild types. What goes on here?

A bias for the blue-eyed and golden-haired, as pure and virtuous, is almost universal. Just think of all the fairy tale princesses, or Bizet's Carmen and Micaela, of Rapunzel and Goldilocks. When I was a little girl I thought it unfair that I could never be a princess because I was neither blue-eyed nor blonde. But here is a song which gives brown eyes their due.

And perhaps we should give the maligned black-eye-Susans their due as well. Many people call them weeds, and in some areas they are enough of a threat to agriculture that farmers must plow them under. But they are not obstreperous; they have their charms. And in a garden they are not difficult to handle. They add color to the roadside or in the garden, blooming during the hot and dry months of July and August, and into fall. And in a vase, they look surprisingly elegant.

Their care is minimal. They want sun, but don't need to be watered, or fertilized, or dead headed. If you wish you can seed them, in fall or very early spring, and transplant the seedlings, but why bother. Let them grow where they will, unless it is an utterly unsuitable spot, and then pull them out. It is that simple.

Black-eye-Susan is a native American plant. It started in the Western prairies and then spread eastwards and naturalized alongside roads. Today it can be found from Florida to Texas to as far north as Labrador. The botanical name is Rudebeckia hirta and it is related to various other cone flowers and daisies. Hirta grows to 2 - 3 feet tall. There is also a slightly larger brown-eyed-Susan, Rudebeckia triloba, which grows to 3-5 feet. Both of them are biennials; their seeds germinate in late summer, grow into new plants which live through the winter and bloom the next year. Without fail.

Yes, they are constant - they are, as the song says: "Ochi czorne, ochi vyorne," black eyes, faithful eyes.

SQUASH

Squashes have interesting mating habits. They are not exactly discriminating, and cannot say "No". Which sometimes leads to unusual offspring. I thought about this when I was rummaging in the jungle by the compost pile and came across a huge cucurbit plant. It was some sort of a squash - which, however, I did not plant there.

The leaves were like standard squash and the yellow blossoms too, but the fruit was something else: about six inches in diameter (the size of a very small cantaloupe), but slightly pear shaped, and greenish yellow with dark green stripes. There were ten of those stripes, and they were the exact color and type as one finds on a zucchini.

Ever curious I decided to cook the squash to see how it tasted. It was good. When I baked it the pale green flesh was moist and had nice flavor. Stir fried with some shallots and lots of herbs it tasted like patty cake squash. Finally I took a large specimen and with some other veggies and herbs, made a squash puree out of it. That too was delicious.

But I still did not know what kind of a squash it was or who were its parents. Obviously it was an illegitimate squash, probably offspring of a zucchini - viz. the stripes - and something else, possibly a winter squash. Shall we say - a May - September mésalliance?

But this is the way squashes and other cucurbits behave. Left to their own devices they cross pollinate with other squashes, or even melons, and next year produce various combinations of the parental genes. As in life, this random coupling is sometimes good and sometimes bad. This was one of the more successful ones. Usually the self seeded plants grow well but the fruit is bland and smaller than its parents.

Which is what one should expect, nature being more interested in quantity than quality. Studies show that with humans, genius IQ parents are likely to have perfectly ordinary children. It is called return to the mean. With the squash it is a return to some Ur-squash.

But, unless you plan to save your seeds for next year's planting, this is only of academic interest. Store boughten' seeds of squashes are civilized, they come out true and uniform. And every proper garden should have at least a plant or two. You need not buy a new packet of seeds every year. Squash seeds remain viable for four to five years.

In July and August summer squashes are in their glory. They need warm, even hot weather to do well. There is no point in seeding or planting them until the soil is at least 60F, and of course the first frost will kill them. They also require full sun, and lots of water, but not on the leaves because this encourages mildew. They are heavy feeders. The soil where they are grown should be enriched with organic materials and fertilized several times during their growing season.

With summer squashes it is usually a deluge or famine. Each

plant can produce huge amounts - unless it dies. There are two pests which cause the worst damage: the squash vine borer and the squash bug, also known as stink bug. Both of them come out early in the season, and can kill the whole plant. One way to fool them is to start a second planting in late June after they are out of the way.

The borers are white caterpillars, about an inch long. They chew their way into the base of the plant, leaving behind sort of a sawdust pile. It is possible to slit the stem and dig them out, then pile soil around the cut so the stem can develop more roots. But it is better to look for the eggs before they hatch and remove them. The adult borer is an orange-black wasplike moth. It lays eggs at the base of the stems, just below the surface, usually in June. The eggs are red-orange, and very tiny - 1/25th of an inch. Some people also cover the growing plants with a light fabric during the egg laying season, so the moths cannot get to them.

The grayish brown squash bugs are 3/4 " long, and their red-brown eggs are attached to the undersides of leaves. Picking them off is one option. Laying a board on the ground for the night is another. The bugs will crawl under it and in the morning they can be destroyed. You can also interplant the area with marigolds, nasturtiums or radishes, which repel squash bugs.

By the way, squashes have both male and female flowers, so those first few blossoms you get on your plants which just drop off and do not form fruit are perfectly normal. They are male and they always come first. The difference between them is that the female blossoms have sort of a waist indentation, and a four-part pistil in the flower's center. The female flowers do the heavy lifting and develop into squashes. I don't know, maybe there is a moral in that.

SUNFLOWERS

It has happened again. Not one of the sunflower seeds I have planted this spring has come up - but I have sunflowers nevertheless. I assume the birds took care of it. I certainly would miss them. There is nothing more cheerful than a bunch of big yellow sunflowers looking at you and at the sun. The smaller side shoots can be used in flower arrangements, the big flowers saved for seeds. And the birds love them.

This year I planted sunflowers by the smoke house. It seemed like a good idea, perhaps because several years ago they grew there and looked just so right against the old logs. But not one of them came up. Only weeds.

I don't know why, I scattered a lot of seeds there. Did the mice get them? Or the birds? Or were the seeds too old to germinate? Perhaps they were washed out after a rainstorm, after all it is on a slope. I don't have an idea, but I do know that there is not a single sunflower growing in that bed.

On the other hand there are two sunflowers in front of the big cabin, one on each side of the door, making it picture perfect. And another really big one is by the dog kennels. That it is there at all is remarkable; that it grew so big with perhaps dozen side shoots is a miracle. That place is never watered and is thoroughly trampled by the animals. Plus there are other sunflowers here and there. Who planted them is a mystery but I don't care. I don't mind being surprised.

But sunflowers are not to be trifled with. They grow big. When the Spanish conquistadors first saw them in South America they were amazed. These were not entirely wild flowers. The Incas had bred them for the fibers, seeds, and flower petals, from which they extracted yellow dye. They also carved their designs on temples. In 1569, in the first book about flora of the New World, sunflower was described as a, "Hearbe of the Sunne.... a straunge flower, for it casteth out the greatest flowers, and the most perticulars that hath been seen, for it is greater than a greate Platter or Dishe..."

European gardeners took to the plant and started a race who could grow the biggest one. The English botanist, John Gerard, in his 1597 "Herbal" wrote that, "It hath risen up to height of fourteene foote in my garden, where one flower was in weight three pound and two ounces." But that was nothing compared to the Madrid's Royal Garden claim, that their sunflower grew to twenty feet. Then the Italians trumped them by boasting that in Padua grew a forty-foot plant.

This might be too much of a good thing. Who would want to have a forty foot sunflower towering over the house, other than registering it for the Guinness world record. Even twenty feet seems excessive. I like them just tall enough so I can reach the flower without having to look for a step ladder.

As a rule sunflowers are easy to grow - except in my case. They should be planted on a sunny site, but not where they would shade other plants. They are drought tolerant but it helps to mulch them to preserve moisture and discourage weeds.

If you don't want the birds to get your seeds cover the flowers with mesh bags or cheesecloth. You can harvest as soon as the backs of the heads turn yellow, and seeds start turning brown. Hang the heads to dry. An easy way to remove the seeds is to rub two seed heads together. Let the loose seeds dry out on screens before storing them. For eating, rather than feeding them to birds, soak the seeds overnight in water, drain, and then roast in a shallow baking sheet for 3 hours at 200F, or until crisp. If you prefer salty nuts, use strong salt water for soaking.

These days we have a choice of many different varieties of sunflowers, some tall as the original and others table size. And not all of them are yellow or have big seeds. In years past I have grown copper colored, almost white, and double petaled flowers of various sizes, and this year I have a row of red Mexican sunflowers that look like zinnias.

But there is much to be said for your basic yellow sunflower whether it is planted by you or the birds. In its full glory it unabashedly celebrates the sun - which is why it is called, "Helianthus," after helios, the sun, and anthos, a flower.

DESIGNER PLANTS

Great-aunt Anna was a modern woman. Although she was born in the 19th century, she was emancipated, traveled widely, and when she was in her late 80s, still drove herself every year from Wisconsin to Florida, and back. But she had firm standards - which she upheld. One of them was not to be used for a billboard.

This came up one day when she was seen picking at her new knit shirt with manicure scissors, unraveling something. When asked, she said impatiently: "Oh there is this stupid alligator, and I am trying to get it off."

When told that the 'stupid alligator' showed the shirt was by the French designer Lacoste, then at the height of his popularity, she was unimpressed. She liked the shirt but she did not like advertising the guy who made it, and although she did not mind paying the price she certainly did not want that information to get around. (This was also before cheap knock-offs with the logo were available on street corners.)

But things have changed since then. Today

it is 'if you have it flaunt it', and designer labels are emblazoned large, front and back, so that even someone with weak eyesight, too vain to wear glasses, can immediately tell what is what.

And of course it is not only shirts but everything else. My sneakers have three logos on each shoe, and another on the soles. So do my sheets and towels, although not so blatantly. Which is a blessing. I'd hate to sleep on a pillow slip with large 'Porthault' embroidered on it. It would make an impression on my cheek and I would be branded for the rest of the day. But such is the trend. Today the manufacturers are selling the sizzle, not the steak.

Selling of brands, rather than the object itself, is now getting even into gardening. Yes, there always have been brands, the venerable Burpee seed company has been around since 1876, Park Seed since 1868, and England's Thompson & Morgan since 1855. But they pushed their wares, not their name.

The original use of brand names was a guarantee: this is who we are and we stand behind our product. It was a contract between the seller and the buyer, not a show for the public. That made sense. But when the brand becomes more important than the product, it is time to worry.

We don't have petunias with little logos on their leaves yet, but we may be getting there. Take gardens by Martha Stewart. It is all coordinated, often pre-planted, and all you do is buy it. What is being offered is packaging, the Martha Stewart lifestyle.

People are taking notice. The news magazine "The Economist" had a cover story on brands and logos and what they stand for. And a book by Naomi Klein "No Logo: Taking Aim at the Brand Bullies," was translated into seven languages. Klein says that the brand has greater value than the product itself and brings in the profits. Some companies spend more on advertising than on production. The Economist tries to look at the bright side, pointing out that as long as there is competition, consumers can take it or leave it. Brands simplify choices, guarantee quality, and, as part of the advertising, provide us with all sorts of free entertainment and amusements -which I think is debatable.

I am a no-logo but not anti brand person. Just like great aunt

Anna, I prefer my shirts without the alligator. So if Martha Stewart comes out with better seeds than Burpee, I will buy them. But count me out if Ralph Lauren starts selling a "Polo Primrose", color- coordinated to his spring collection, with a discreet "RL" on the stem. That is where I draw the line.

WHY BOTHER ?

Why bother? Lately this was going through my mind as I was coping with the summer crush; a stream of house guests, completing paperwork on two hundred historic surveys I did last winter, before I get to the next batch this fall, as well as inquiries about progress on a stalled editing work. Don't ask about that - too painful - the computer ate my notes.

And then the garden - demanding immediate and complete attention. Looking at it I thought of a Japanese poem written more than a thousand years ago: "The flowers withered, Their color faded away, While meaninglessly, I spent my days in the world."

Yes indeed. While I was spending my days in the world the flowers were not only withering, they were fading into whitish gray. Especially the phloxes. They were coming down with powdery mildew. This was just too much.

Late summer gardens are never at their best, unless one is fond of weeds, but phloxes usually hold up. Their white, pink, and scarlet spikes do not wilt in the heat, and a bit of drought does not matter. But humidity, and off and on drizzle is their enemy. Soon leaves develop brown splotches and the tell tale white sheen of mildew. And then they curl up and die.

The type of mildew which attacks them is found also on lilacs, melons, and cucumbers, so it is hard to control. Prevention is easier than cure. This is because spores of the mold are blown by wind to other plants, and will over winter in infected leaves left on the ground.

It is possible to spray the mildewed plants with sulfur every week, and this may stop it. But disposing of all infected plants is even more effective. This does not mean dumping it on the compost pile - bag it or burn it. Prevention includes using mildew free plants, and giving them room enough, so that air and sun can get to them. In wet weather preventive use of sulfur, before mildew develops, is also helpful.

I knew all this but it got away from me. Now the only course of action was to remove the diseased plants and protect the few healthy specimen from getting contaminated. This was going to be a hot and itchy job. This is when I thought: 'Why bother', and went inside to solace myself with the latest issue of Vogue.

I find Vogue diverting, especially articles about the lives of fashion icons. The effort these people put into being on the cutting edge is astounding. Before they go to a function, women will spend several hours on their make-up, and that does not include styling their hair. Then there are the clothes - from little T-shirts at couple of hundred dollars each, to couturier gowns costing as much as a top line automobile. In some places it could buy you a modest house. Is this vanity or what? Why do they bother? It seems so much work. I compared it to the common public grunge, where clothes fine for cleaning out the barn are seen in stores, at airports, in restaurants, because people want to be comfortable and don't care what anyone thinks of them. Is this virtue or not?

Mulling it over I reluctantly came to the conclusion that the grunge was vanity. It said: others don't count, I don't owe them anything, the world owes me. The fashion slaves are more civilized as they try to create something ephemeral and give it to the world. They are less arrogant than the others.

Hey, you take inspiration where you find it, and go with it. It means that with my phloxes I cannot plow them under, I have to bother. I owe it to the world, even though my garden is not important and few people get to see it. It is the civilized thing to do. And so I am doing it.

TAIL END OF SUMMER

At the tail end of summer I want to hit the rewind button and start all over again. There is nothing wrong with fall but not so soon. The garden may be saying "enough already" but I think, " you mean no more swimming? How will I survive?" and shout "Lets go back to June."

The daily swim, and even more days which start in daylight and end with long lazy afternoons, and not having to wear long pants, are the good life. They put me in a mood to do what needs to be done. Energy breeds more energy while lassitude brings on the blahs.

Of course we all know that wishing does not make it so, and the short, crisp days of fall are coming whether we are ready for them or not, to be followed by winter. Even I realize it and wonder if plants can feel the same. Most of them are ready to call it a year and settle down for a winter's rest. Some of them show signs of it as early as August. My weeping cherries started dropping leaves and turning color some weeks ago.

The perennials have gone through their annual cycle leaving behind dry stalks of lilies and daisies and yarrow, or sparsely blooming spikes of phloxes above mottled leaves. Even the annuals are giving up no matter how much you deadhead or cut them. Their foliage gets tired looking, and mildew sets in.

But there are other plants just getting into stride. The dahlias among them. No matter how early in the summer they start blooming, their best flowers are reserved for fall, and the very best the week of the first frost. They show bravado. Given a mild fall they'd bloom till Christmas.

Chrysanthemums are not like that. If they start early they finish early. It used to irritate me to have them bloom in July and turn brown and ragged by September. Only the late mums stick around through couple of minor frosts, although at this point they are not worth cutting and taking inside. But I would like to say a good word about the small marigolds. They too start blooming in early summer, and keep at it with renewed energy until hard frost. I usually manage to keep a few until Thanksgiving.

By Thanksgiving I am slowly getting resigned to the change of seasons, and even enjoying some of it, but not totally. Unlike in my youth when fall meant being a year older, a new school year, and usually a new boyfriend, all that is left now is the first. Getting older is not what it used to be, after a while it loses its charm, and utility. I do have a drivers license and no one has carded me for ages.

Summer is for children, winter is to be an adult. That sounded tempting once. But over the years I came to the conclusion that adulthood is overrated. I don't do adult, certainly not willingly - or convincingly. In summer I don't have to.

FALL

Fall is an ambivalent time. There are the happy memories and there are the regrets. The two probably cancel each other out.

At the beginning of fall the garden still has much to offer, the last tomatoes, the first fall crocus and many other things as well. You may wish you had staked those floppy chrysanthemums, so they would not spill all over everything. And you most certainly regret not planting a fall crop of dill, lettuce or spinach, and promise to do so next year.

By the time the autumn winds and rains and chills arrive, you don't care if goldenrod is going mano a mano with the spreading shasta daisies, or what are the funny looking weeds that have taken over the flowerbeds. You long for a couple of hard frosts to take care of it and let you start all over with a clean slate next spring.

AUTUMN

Whether you call it Fall or Autumn it is the time of the year when night absorbs light at both sides of the day. Things get dark and dismal and our spirits sink.

But nature is merciful. To ease the transition she gives us a short period of exuberant, riotous color, before the winter gets its grip on us, and our bones get chilled. And, if the weather cooperates, this period when trees change from green to yellows, oranges and reds, can be the loveliest time of the year.

This is the time for poets - and scientists - they both have a lot to say about it. I rather suspect that the poets understand it better, but the scientists are expanding their knowledge with new research. They do it from plain curiosity but also because some of it may be of practical use.

It has been long known that the leaf color changes are triggered by the shorter days and colder temperatures breaking down chlorophyll which makes the leaves green. As the chlorophyll is removed it allows the other colors to be seen. These colors are called carotenoids and they are the various shades of yellows, ambers and oranges. Different trees have varying amounts of carotenoids which explains the many shades of the leaves. But the carotenoids cannot produce the red colored leaves.

So, what causes the reds? For a long time this was a mystery. Finally, several groups of scientists came up with an explanation. A different pigment makes leaves turn red, purple or magenta. This is anthocyanin which is not part of the leaf, but is newly created in fall, probably through environmental changes. And it has a distinct purpose. The red, being relatively dark, shades the leaf from excessive light.

It seems strange to worry about light, or anything, with a leaf which is about to fall off the tree, but it does matter. Leaves gather nutrients and send them down to the rest of the tree so it can survive and grow. If leaves fall off prematurely the tree has less nutrients stored to carry it through the winter.

The idea that red leaves are there to shade the tree was already proposed in the 19th century, but the how and why was not clear. Recently the scientists came up with connection between the red color and the amount of sunlight, that the more exposed leaves get redder. Also how the timing for leaves turning red is related to how much of nutrition remains in the leaves and needs to be shifted to the tree. This explains why some years have fabulous fall foliage while other years are so so. The whole process is obviously more complicated. It is also about nitrogen and sugars, which are the good guys, and peroxides and free radicals which are bad, and how these molecules manage to stow the energy gathered by chlorophyll into storage for winter.

One reason behind the study was utilitarian, because knowing when leaves turn can have commercial value. In many states fall foliage tourism is big business and everyone wants to know when the best colors are likely to appear. Alas, despite all the new data, we still cannot predict it for sure. Nature is not a laboratory, there are too many variables.

As it often happens, research explains everything and nothing, or so it seems. But poets do understand the true meaning of fall. And only they know how to express the bittersweet feeling of loss we feel as another year ends.

> "I see the messenger come
> As the yellow leaves are falling.
> Oh, well I remember
> How on such a day we used to meet --"

So speaks an ancient Japanese poet in the Collection of Ten Thousand Leaves". And isn't this all we need to know?

QUINCE

Come September, the fruit on the quince begins to ripen. It is still hard, but the color changes from green to pale yellow. If I have time and the spirit moves me, I start thinking about making quince butter. If I wait until after the first frost the fruit will turn brown and mushy and unusable.

I am talking about the fruiting quince (genus Cydonia) which is a thornless and deciduous tree 15 to 20 feet tall. There are named varieties of the fruiting Cydonia quince and some nurseries carry them. These are different from the flowering quince (Chaenomeles), which is a shrub with white or dark pink flowers used in ornamental planting.

My quince is the basic, common quince. It was a favorite of 19-century maidens because of the early spring blossoms. It marked for them the end of long, dark winters and promised better days to come, offering beauty and hopes of romance. (With romance the whole world is seen as beautiful, while with beauty, even though it is in the eye of the beholder, quality counts.)

My tree is a magnificent specimen - over 15 feet tall and more than that wide. In spring it has single petaled white flowers which can be forced to bloom inside in late winter. In fall it is covered with hundreds of velvety round fruits that look like a cross between a pear and an apple. I don't know how old it is, but quinces live a long time, so it may easily date into the 19th century. Whatever its age it is hale and hearty, growing up and out, and sprouting little shoots at its base. Every few years I have to give it a drastic pruning so it does not take over that end of the garden.

Other than that it does not need much care. Quince trees do best in rich, moist loam, but they will grow in any garden soil. They can be attacked by leaf blight or mildew, and a few years ago the Japanese beetles made their headquarters there. But other than a temporary partial defoliation my tree survived it all.

I have been always fond of quinces - but until I moved here only in the abstract. I had never seen one, much less tasted one. All I had to go on was Edward Lear's The Owl and the Pussycat, "wherein they dined on mince and slices of quince, which they ate with a runcible spoon." That tickled my imagination.

Reality set in when I finally bit into one. Raw quince is one of the tartest fruits I have ever tasted. (I wonder whether Mr. Lear knew that.) If you try it, even your teeth will pucker. But it has culinary uses. Fannie Farmer, in her Boston Cooking School book, has a recipe for baked quinces. These are cooked whole, in the oven, with plenty of sugar.

Quince is also very high in pectin, the stuff which makes jams and jellies thicken, and was used for that before commercial pectin became common. Cooked, with lots of sugar, it can be used in pies and tarts and it makes interesting jelly or butter. The taste is a little like apple but with a different aroma.

I make my quince butter in the microwave rather than on top of the stove. This saves all the stirring and prevents scorching. I prepare the fruit the same way as for apple butter and then cook it in small batches on full power in 10 - to 15 - minute intervals until it is the right consistency. I will flavor it with various spices, or other fruits such as a few plums, and add some sherry or port wine to it.

Perhaps the owl and the pussycat had their slices of quince stewed. But it couldn't have been too runny because a runcible spoon is sort of a pierced spoon, or as my dictionary defines it: a sharp-edged fork with three broad curved prongs.

BIMBOS

There are bimbos and then there are thinking man's bimbos. Don't laugh, thinking man's bimbos really exist. This hit me recently in the gym, as I was mechanically moving my legs on the treadmill, unsuccessfully trying to ignore the television. I wondered about the essence of bimboism and what was its appeal.

Dictionaries are no help. They report how the word has been used, ranging from (1) the female posterior - which must be an archaic use, (2) blonde of limited talent and limitless ambition - better, and (3) someone who lusts after fame and fortune - which covers too big a field. There is more to it than that because none of it mentions the universal attraction of bimbos. Which is why we have more than one kind of them. About the thinking man's brand more later, first about flower bimbos.

The most obvious example of that are chrysanthemums. Not your common pot of mums sold in every nursery, but the big, showy football mums. People love them. They are magnificent, spectacular, and don't seem to be quite of this world. But they are - it is all in the grooming. They start plebeian, just regular florists chrysanthemums, and proceed from there. It takes a fair amount of work. To get the big long stemmed beauties you carefully disbud young chrysanthemums, leaving just one bud per stem. In due time, with proper care, staking and feeding, you have your eye catching football mums.

One problem is that these chrysanthemums are not dependably winter hardy, and do better in the greenhouse than in the garden. And even if you carry them through the winter, age does not agree with them. Next year's blooms tend to be smaller no matter what you do. The only way to keep them is to start new plants from cuttings taken from roots, in late fall, and then overwinter them in a frost-free greenhouse or cold frame. Not unlike the human bimbos, whatever variety. They too are made, not born. It all is in the intent and grooming.

But what is the difference between the usual Hollywood or girlie magazines bimbo and an upscale one found more likely in New York? We know a bimbo when we see one. Or do we? The essence of bimbo-ism is in the artifice - pure and simple. With regular bimbos it is impossible to miss, shouting loud "Here I am, a work of art, notice me!" Thinking man's bimbo uses a softer voice, but everything else is the same.

Well, not quite same. Instead of curves, often surgically enhanced, there are planes and angles, even more often the work of a surgeon. To be a thinking man's bimbo takes a size 2 figure, a pert slightly upturned nose, and finely crafted cheekbones, plus, if you don't want to look common, no blond hair. The new must-have-color is what we used to call Titian red, after the 16th century Venetian painter. It is dark brown with an undertone of crimson, and it must be straight.

Most of us do not aspire to bimboism - perhaps because we have no hope of succeeding, just think about the cost of it - but bimboism is not bad. It is quite attractive, and can be amusing, unless you find yourself surrounded by it. In some circles, where plastic surgeons sculpt identical faces, shall we say Model Di#2, on their clients, and hair colorists hit the very same shade, it is like seeing a bunch of clones. It becomes boring.

The same goes for the football mums. Maybe a few of them in a vase, but a little bit of that goes a long way. I prefer my chrysanthemums slightly disheveled, even falling over, and in all sorts of colors. I like the spoon varieties best of all. They don't take themselves seriously.

POTATOES

You know the game where someone says a word and you have to say the first thing that comes to your mind? The word I have in mind is 'potato.' How you answer could tell a lot about you.

If you answer 'famine' you are into history. 'Beetle' pegs you as a gardener. 'Fries' suggests working at a fast food place. 'Mashed' may mean either the dance or food for babies. Or you could say, latkes, vichyssoise, Mr. Potato Head, or Dan Qayle. The choices are many. My answer is 'the Incas'.

The reason? I have just returned from the High Andes where the Incas lived and where potatoes originated. At an altitude of 10,000 feet or more corn would not grow, or much else. So they terraced the steep barren mountains and planted potatoes. The Inca empire is long since gone, but their potato fields are still there. In the 16th century when the Spanish conquistadors came to plunder the Inca land of its gold, they also picked up a few spuds as souvenirs. The rest is history.

Before long, the potato became ubiquitous. It would grow in soil too poor for anything else and in almost any climate. It improved the nutrition of the people and drove the population growth, especially in Ireland. (It was probably Sir Walter Raleigh or Francis Drake who brought it to England.)

But there was a down side to this. Although most years the potato harvest was plentiful it could fail. The big 1845-46 potato blight in Ireland was not the first or only one, there had been several other crop failures in the 18th century and the early part of the 19th. These too were caused by fungal and viral diseases. Luckily they did not spread as widely. Even today potatoes are susceptible to fungal and bacterial blights although resistant varieties are being developed. And fortunately we are no longer dependent on them for our survival.

Today it may seem silly to be growing potatoes when for couple of dollars there are bags of them in the supermarket - all clean and ready to pop into a pot. But the selection is limited. If you want something more interesting, a potato that can stand on its own without large additions of butter or gravy, you may want to grow your own. I am especially fond of the little fingerlings. The Yukon Gold are also delicious with their thicker skin and yellow flesh. And there are others. Some are early ripening, some late, some will keep but others should be eaten soon.

To grow potatoes you start with 'seed potatoes.' They are available at farm and garden supply stores or through catalogs. Cut them up so that each section has one or two eyes which will sprout into a new plant. Before planting, you can let each cut piece dry slightly, spread in an airy place for 24 hours. Early maturing potatoes should be planted two to three weeks before last frost, late March to early April in our part of Virginia. The late ripening can be planted through mid June. They should be able to mature before the first fall frost.

Make rows about three feet apart, and space the potatoes at least six inches apart. Cover them with four or five inches of soil. Potatoes grow best in sandy soil, with heavy clay you can use mulch to cover them. As the plants come up cover them with more soil, leaves or mulch. The developing potatoes will form around the roots and should not be exposed to sunlight. Sun turns them green and mildly toxic. Besides, leaving a smaller part of the vines exposed encourages root development.

When plants bloom stop hilling the soil, but apply mulch to conserve moisture and discourage weeds. Also watch for potato beetles - the tan striped bugs that lay yellow eggs on the underside of the leaves. They hatch into reddish larvae with voracious appetites. There are sprays and dusts to take care of them but picking the bugs and larvae off and drowning them in soapy water works as well. It depends how many potatoes you are growing. You can try it if you have couple of rows. Don't do it with couple of acres, because either your back or your knees - or both - will give out. To discourage bugs and other diseases that overwinter in the soil potato plantings should be rotated each year, and not put in the same spot.

You can harvest your first young potatoes shortly after the plants start to bloom. These will be rather small. The potatoes are fully ripe when the foliage dies, but they will keep in ground for several weeks. Dig them up with a spading fork before the first frost. Store them in a cool dark place, in basement or root cellar. Or you can keep them in baskets, covered with newspapers, but check them occasionally and throw out any that rot or turn green.

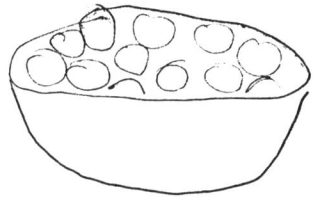

Potatoes are good for you. They have large amounts of vitamins A, B-1, B-2, C and potassium, and if you don't drown them in butter they are low in calories. The best way to enjoy the first young potatoes is to boil them in their skins and serve them topped with butter and cottage cheese seasoned with salt, pepper and a generous amount of chopped chives. A bowl of that makes very satisfying supper.

CAULIFLOWER

Cauliflower - Mark Twain called it a cabbage with college education, which perhaps fit when precious few people went to college, and not many ate the vegetable. Today I might call it a cabbage with sex appeal.

Yes, cauliflower belongs into the cabbage family, which becomes obvious when you cook it. - the smell is unmistakable. But in all other respects it is in a class of its own. This queen of vegetables is decidedly glamorous, and fall is the best season for it.

When I say queen I am not kidding. I am barely stretching the point. It was Madame du Barry, the mistress of Louis XV, who put it on the culinary map by giving her name to a cauliflower soup - Creme Dubarry. This became the favorite at the French court, and later when the court was no longer, of those who survived the Revolution.

I have been unable to find the exact recipe for 'Creme Dubarry.' None of my cookbooks lists it and only few include any kind of cauliflower soup. The Gourmet cookbook has a version with rice, which somehow doesn't look right, and Fannie Farmer has a cream of cauliflower which seems closer.

But making cauliflower soup is no rocket science. It is made with sautéed onions or leeks, crushed or pureed cauliflower either with vegetable stock or chicken stock, plus some cream or béchamel sauce. The only question is how much texture it should have. Should it be pureed smooth or should little bits of cauliflower float in it. Either way is good. Our cook Tonchi went the smooth route and then thickened it with an egg yolk or two. That can be tricky because it must be added carefully, mixed in some of the warm, but not hot soup, so it does not curdle. But this gives it a special smoothness. I suspect that Tonchi's soup was the real 'Creme Dubarry.'

If making cauliflower soup is easy, growing it is not. It wants pampering. Cauliflower is a cool weather vegetable, needing at least two months of cool weather to mature. Some varieties require more than that.

When fully grown cauliflower will tolerate a bit of frost but hot weather suits it not. The trick is to find the right variety for the climate, and hope that the weather will not do something weird like freeze in June or get boiling hot in October.

In our area cauliflower should be started inside in early spring, four to six weeks before the last frost. The seedlings will need sun, or a good source of light, and constant moisture. In the south the seeds can be planted outside to over-winter for spring harvest.

Once set outside the plants must have at least one inch of water a week - without fail. If they dry out the crowns will turn 'ricey,' meaning they will separate instead of forming a solid ball. Also the crowns must be kept shaded so they will stay white instead of turning purple or green or some other unappetizing color.

The best way to shade them is by tying their leaves up on the top like an upturned collar. This must be done on a dry day so no moisture is left on the crown. If wet it may lead to rot. This is also the reason for untying the heads from time to time, especially after rain, to let the crown dry out, and to check for bugs. And, of course, after the heads are tied all watering should be done just around the roots and not over the top. Care must be taken with cultivating because if roots get damaged the plant will develop unevenly. Feeding should be with fish emulsion fertilizer or manure tea every three to four weeks.

Cauliflower probably arrived from the Middle East. In the 17th century it appeared in France and England and from there it came to America. However, other than for soups, it was not well known or popular. The problem may have been the customary way of cooking it, by boiling it at great length, until it lost all shape and taste.

The Victorians had something called 'chou-fleur a l'eau,' which is a fancy way of describing a cauliflower mush. That sounds thoroughly unappetizing, but for some strange reason people used to fear under-cooked, or raw vegetables. These were only for animals, food for people had to be boiled into submission. Today we know better and enjoy our cauliflower al dente or raw. The crunchiness is the best part of the taste.

ORNAMENTAL CABBAGE

They have beguiling colors, shocking pink, purple, creamy white, set off by muted green. They display their ruffled edges like a bunch of deeply bowing ballerinas. Even their names sound like poetry: Nagoya, Tokyo, Peacock, Rose Bouquet, Pink Beauty, and White Christmas. There is nothing stodgy about them. They happily brighten your fall garden through the early frosts into winter.

I am talking about ornamental cabbages or kale. In addition to being ornamental, they are also pretty good to eat. That is sometimes a disadvantage - but more of that later. The leaves just beg to be used as garnish, under cold meat, or incorporated in salads. Every garden should have some, whether in beds, or containers, or window boxes. If you do not grow any, you may be able to find some in a nursery or garden store. But really, they are easy to grow from seed, if you start early.

I start my ornamental cabbage seeds in late May or June, when all the other seedlings I have been fussing over are in the ground and fending for themselves, and my seed starting trays are empty again ready to be reused. According to directions the seeds should germinate in 14 to 21 days, but I have had them showing up in little over a week. After that spindly little shoots appear. They are content in the seed tray until they get their first four to six real leaves, when they want to be moved into larger pots.

Depending on the size of pots the cabbages can stay in them, or later be moved into still larger containers, or into flower beds. In beds they should be 14 to 16 inches apart. If they get too leggy it is fine to plant them deeper into ground, new roots will grow in the buried portion. It will take at least three months for them to develop, even for the quicker varieties. Most likely they will not start doing much until cooler weather,

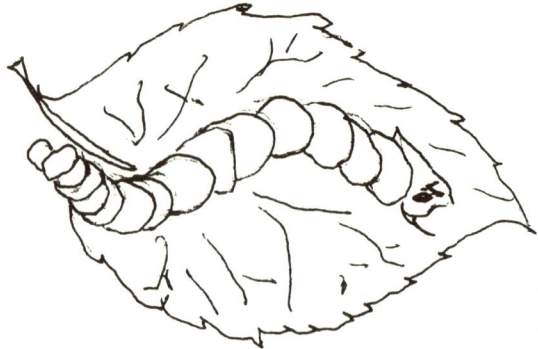

in September or October. Unless the soil is rich they appreciate fertilizer which is especially important if they are grown in pots. Once a month outside and more often if in pots is about right. They develop their best color when night temperatures fall into the 50F. After that it is plain sailing.

But ornamental cabbages are not totally trouble free. As mentioned, they are tasty. And there is the rub. I have planted as many as thirty cabbage seedlings only to find a few days later twenty seven bare, twisted, pale green stems, totally devoid of any leaves, and perhaps three survivors, a bit tattered, but still showing some life.

The first time this happened I was at loss to account for it. The plants were in a flower bed, in the open. Was it the slugs? Well, maybe. There were some around and they can strip a small plant of leaves overnight. So I started vigorously eradicating them - with modest results. The cabbages lived, but were not much to brag about, their tutus did not look like they belonged to ballerinas but more like they came from my daughter's dress-up box.

Next year I decided to keep my cabbages in pots, on the terrace, away from any slugs - but much the same thing happened. Instead of pretty ruffles they developed holes in their leaves. On close observation I found all sorts of minute cabbage worms, smaller than a tip of a pencil. But those little guys had big appetites, doubling their size about every twelve hours. I picked them off, and washed them off, spending a ridiculous amount of time on it, only to find a new bunch of caterpillars each next day.

I was becoming convinced that the caterpillars came packaged with the seeds - sort of just add soil and water and you too will have a large crop of green caterpillars. Finally in desperation I used Diazon insect spray. It worked. Some garden manuals suggest using BT (Bacillus thuringiensis) which is totally nontoxic to people and animals and completely safe. I may try that next year.

CHRYSANTHEMUMS

November is that time of the year for autumnal melancholy and regrets for things not done. Time is running out, year is ending, and we wake up each morning to darkness.

No one understands this better than Japanese poets. They approach it obliquely, yet nail it down in a couple of lines. "Did you not know beforehand, that all the things must fade away?", asks one, long since dead writer, while another sums it up with, "A pine-cricket, all in vain is chirping now, In my weed-grown house."

But not all is sadness. If the fragile cherry blossoms define Japanese spring, it is the sturdy chrysanthemum which brightens their fall. And ours too. Without chrysanthemums my garden would be totally weed-grown now. And there would be nothing to brighten my house.

Yet I have ambivalent feelings about chrysanthemums. I associate them with All Souls' Day, which comes near Halloween (November 2) but has little in common with it. Halloween is kids, dressing up, pranks, candy, and trick and treating. All Souls Day is visiting graves at the cemetery and decorating them with flowers and lighted candles.

Growing up I lived in Prague, the capital of Czech Republic, near the large cemetery Olsany, which was surrounded by flower seller stalls. Each fall these stalls overflowed with potted and cut chrysanthemums in many colors - but it is their scent which I remember best. Chrysanthemums, under some circumstances, perhaps dampness or cold, develop a distinct smell, not pleasant but not unpleasant.

Unlike the smell of fallen leaves, which is a joyful part of autumn, the smell of chrysanthemums is essence of the dying year. Even today, when I arrange them for the hall table, I am taken back. I am ten years old, walking through Olsany in the fall's early darkness, surrounded by the spirits of the dead. But I grow chrysanthemums and would not consider a garden complete without them. Some have been started from seed, others came as slips from a friend's garden, and a few I bought.

I am not terribly fond of the cushion mums, those sold by nurseries, which look like a ball of color. Nothing wrong with that, if that is what you want. But these are useless for flower arranging and when they finish blooming they do it all at once and it is a sorry sight. Also they seldom survive till next year, or if they do they look ragged. Buying small plants early in the season is usually a better choice.

I have had good experience starting chrysanthemums from seeds. Except for the fanciest types which can be temperamental, they are easy to grow, and will provide flowers the first year if they are started early enough. Most seed companies carry both annual and perennial types. The seeds often come as mixed selections, so that you don't end up with one hundred plants of the same color - which obviously is to be avoided unless you have a large circle of gardening friends.

Whether you buy your plants or grow them from seed the trick is to pinch them. When you bring home that single stalk in a little pot, and transplant it into the garden, you must pinch off the top so it will branch. And then do it again and again. Come July stop and let the buds develop. Chrysanthemums need sun, fertilizer early in the season (20-20-20 is good), and regular watering. However, do not apply fertilizer after July. It encourages late growth causing possible winter injury.

There are early blooming chrysanthemums and late blooming types. What makes them bloom is daylight. When days get short enough they bloom. My chrysanthemums are the late blooming kind, which is a mixed blessing. Yes, I have them after most flowers get killed by frost, but if the frost is hard they get nipped too. This happened last year. After a brutal cold spell most of my chrysanthemums were singed even before they opened. They never looked any good. This year they had tight, hard buds at the first frost and were not harmed by it. But since everything else had died, I went through a couple of weeks of no flowers until they deigned to open.

Although chrysanthemums are called hardy, they will not always survive winter, especially in cold areas. What encourages survival are well developed roots which have been watered in fall, and covering the plants with several inches of loose mulch. Also do not cut off the spent flower stalks until spring. They protect the root crowns. After two, three years the plant will need to be divided. Do it in spring when new shoots appear. Dig out the whole clump and slice it into two or more sections and replant these.

Chrysanthemums started in China over 1800 years ago. Couple of hundred years later they came to Japan. The Japanese raised their cultivation to an art form. They thought them as queen of flowers, symbolizing longevity and perseverance. The Chinese were not oblivious to the beauty of chrysanthemums, but being of pragmatic nature they also explored their medicinal use. Soon they discovered that the flowers of the yellow Ju Hua could be dried and made into a refreshing tea. The infusion relieved headaches, fought infections such as colds and flu, and was used to improve eyesight. For tired eyes compresses of warm flower heads were placed on the eyelids.

There may have been something to it. Clinical trials by the Chinese and Japanese, done in the 1970s, showed that Ju Hua infusion was beneficial in lowering blood pressure, relieving headaches, dizziness, and for insomnia.

My highly unscientific opinion is that a cup of warm tea, made with almost anything, has beneficial effects on body and soul. But if you want to experiment with yellow chrysanthemums, steam your flower heads before you dry them to reduce bitterness.

DEER

All right, we all love Bambi. He is so sweet, touching and defenseless - but he is a cartoon - not a live deer. Live deer are much less lovable, especially to a gardener.

Deer in the garden are pests. They can destroy your prize bushes, annihilate the flower garden and lay waste to the vegetable patch. Fences will not stop them. I have seen a posse of deer sail across a pasture fence, a bank, and onto the road, without breaking formation. They are especially bad in early spring when food is still scarce, and again in the fall when they are getting ready for winter. Or if it is dry and the woods are parched. And, of course, in winter when they may even eat bark off the trees. There is really no time of the year when you are safe from them.

Is there nothing that can stop them? Well, yes and no. There are some things that help but nothing is totally effective. The three best defenses are fences, dogs, and planting what they don't like.

If you choose a fence it has to be high, at least 8 feet, or wide, or electrified. A wide fence could be double row, meaning two fences side by side, or it could be slanted, or with an overhang on top, much like jail fences. Deer can clear a high fence or a wide one, but not both at the same time. They also will not jump over a fence if they cannot see through. A solid fence or a wall will deter them even if it is only five feet high. Dogs, especially lively large dogs, also work well. But they cannot be tied up because deer are not stupid. They figure out how far the chain reaches and stay out of that area.

In my years of gardening I have had no problems with deer because I had dogs. Although deer can go from zero to 45 miles per hour in something like 45 seconds, my Labradors could give them a good chase if necessary. And they would bark.

Planting what deer don't like helps but is not foolproof - deer like almost everything. At least some of them do. Individual deer have their preferences and dislikes, but they are not telling us - except by what they eat. Mostly they like what we like. But there are some plants which they usually pass up because of the smell or the texture. Most herbs such as chives, fennel, onions, leeks, rosemary, thyme, marjoram, sweet basil, oregano, parsley, garlic, tarragon are not on their menu. Also asparagus, squash, potatoes, pawpaw, persimmon, myrtle, walnut, and pomegranate. And they will not eat kudzu vine, but that is not a good enough reason to plant it.

Their favorites among flowers are roses, hostas, daylilies, chrysanthemums, and spring bulbs, except daffodils. In vegetables and fruits they like best beans, broccoli, cauliflower, corn, lettuce, peas, strawberries, raspberries, apples and blackberries.

Some people suggest using deterrents, such as hanging scented soaps or dryer fabric softeners on trees, stashing human hair in bags around various plants, spraying foliage with a mixture of rotten eggs and water, or crushed garlic in an old sock. There are also commercial products advertised as deer repellents. All of these will work - sometimes - and only for a while. They have to be replaced or refreshed frequently when the scent dissipates, and sooner or later the deer get used to them and start ignoring them.

Of course deer have their uses, they give us venison. This is mostly of academic interest to us today, which is a pity. Cooked right, venison is delicious. The last time I had it was in Stuttgart in Germany about three years ago. It was at a wonderfully funky place, half restaurant, half an indoor riding rink. As we were eating behind the large windows horses with riders were cantering round and round the rink. And the venison was superb - as were the wild mushrooms served with it.

I have fond memories of our cook Tonchi's way with venison. First she hung it, then marinated it with red wine and herbs, but the secret was in larding it. Venison is lean meat, which tends to cook tough unless it is larded. She had a special larding needle, a narrow tube with one sharp end which she threaded with strips of country bacon. Then she masterfully pushed this through the meat leaving a trail of bacon. This not only tenderized it but gave it more flavor. I have not seen a larding needle for years. I wonder if they still exist.

DOGS IN THE GARDEN

Gardens would not be the same without dogs. How different they would be I don't know because I never had an opportunity to see it. From the time I planted under adult supervision my first radish seeds, there were dogs around to uproot them, and to dig up any other things around.

It is an immutable law of nature that dogs dig. They dig holes, they dig trenches, and dig to expose roots of whatever happens to be growing well. If there is a fence they will dig under it to get to the other side. And if they have something they treasure they will probably hide it under a pile of dirt.

On the subject of that there is a family story known as "Dasha and her loaf of bread." This happened a long time ago. Dasha has since gone to the Happy Doggy Digging Grounds, and is buried under purple bearded iris near the chicken house. However, when she was a puppy we were living on New York's Long Island, which is nothing more than a large sand dune, deposited there eons ago by a glacier, but covered now with highways and houses.

One day I came home with a load of groceries, but as I was putting them away I could not find the bread. We are not talking about plastic wrapped Wonder bread but a yard long loaf of crusty french bread which is definitely too large to be overlooked. I checked the car, looked inside the house and even brought out the sales slip which showed a charge for the bread. But it was nowhere to be found and I had to conclude it must have somehow fallen off the grocery cart while I was not looking, although that seemed unlikely.

About a week later, weeding under bushes, there was a strange lumpy object. When I pried it out, it was a couple of feet of a sand covered french bread. Dear Dasha had gorged on a part of it, but since it was bigger than she was, she could not eat it all and saved the rest for later. How that pup managed to drag it off without anyone seeing it, and then dig a hole large enough to cover it seemed impossible, except that it was not. The evidence was right in front of my eyes.

Except for that Dasha was not the most notorious of my dogs. Hard to say who gets that crown. It is probably a tie between W. William and Christi. W.W. commonly known as Worthless William, earned his name honestly. He was a well rounded dog who excelled not only in digging, but also in climbing over a five foot link fence, attacking neighbors' garbage cans, and even them if they objected and effortlessly getting into trouble. He was the only member of our family, human or otherwise, who ever was under care of a psychiatrist. He needed it and it helped. He too is no longer alive after making a mistake of going down to the road at night. Someone ran over him.

But Christi is very much with us, and I love her, except when she digs. Which is often. She is a hunting dog so she hunts, all sorts of things some of which are to be found underground. Recently she has dug a crater in front of the house, possibly tracking a scent of a groundhog which lived under the old tree stump. We used to have groundhogs on every corner of the garden but since Christi came they have moved out, probably muttering, "There goes the neighborhood."

Then Christi has been working in the hosta patch, looking for mice. The object of interest in the perennial bed below the stone wall I suspect is the snake, or snakes. We do have the usual complement of small garden snakes and a few large black snakes and the dogs don't approve of them at all.

But Christi's masterpiece is a trench, at least 30 feet long leading across the back lawn from the porch to the lower garden steps. I know why it is there. For more years than I care to remember this has been the principal highway for the moles and voles to travel from some ur-nest near the house to the flower beds where I plant my spring bulbs. I myself have been mapping it and filling their tunnels with various noxious things to discourage them, but to no avail. I hope that Christi has better luck. If she succeeds I will gladly forgive her.

WINTER

The dark months of winter lie heavily on the gardener. One wants to be outside doing something but nature thwarts it with cold, snow and frozen ground. Houseplants are not enough. Chasing white flies off the poinsettia, or aphids off the ferns does not satisfy the urge.

Winter gardening demands sublimation. It is virtual gardening. This is a good time to go outside and properly look at the landscape. In winter it shows its bones. The foliage is gone, the color is no longer there, only the bare outlines are visible. This is the time to think about the basics, plan major changes. As the garden catalogs arrive, earlier and earlier each year, you can let your imagination soar. There is plenty of time to become realistic and practical when spring comes.

MISTLETOE

Christmas would not be Christmas without mistletoe. I know this is not exactly what Jo said in the Little Women, but under different circumstance she might have. Christmas and mistletoe belong together.

When mistletoe, Christmas, and kissing teamed up I am not sure, but for centuries it was part of festive rituals the world over. The Druids in England were big on mistletoe. They harvested it with golden sickles and sacrificed white bulls to it. Other ancient people may have used it as well. Pliny the Elder said that mistletoe infusions were a cure for sterility. That was before we had Christmas - or Viagra.

Nicholas Culpeper's mid-17th century Herbal said that the dried mistletoe berry "doth mollify hard knots, tumores and imposthumes (abcesses)," and that a necklace of mistletoe sprigs cures apoplexy and palsy. There were other mentions of its curative powers, but nothing about any romantic possibilities.

This probably did not appear until the 19th century, although there are some precedents, both real and mythological. Legend has it that the Scandinavian god of peace Balder was slain with an arrow made of mistletoe. With the help of other gods his life was restored. Mistletoe was then given to the goddess of love, who decreed that anyone passing under the plant receive a kiss - to show mistletoe was a symbol of love.

Erasmus in the 16th century wrote apropos celebrating the Christmas season: "Turn where you will, there are kisses, kisses everywhere." It is not clear whether he meant it under mistletoe. But somehow, from a simple seasonal decoration, it evolved into the much appreciated Christmas custom of stealing a kiss under it. This was the grand daddy of our social kiss.

No one really cultivates mistletoe. It grows, a parasite, on branches of various trees. There are two varieties, American and European. Although they both look alike, more or less, they are unlike botanically. If they serve the same purpose at Christmas time, medically they are different. What could have worked for Pliny would be dangerous with the American variety. It contains toxic proteins which can slow heart rate, cause hallucinations, convulsion and increase blood pressure. Especially the berries should be kept out of the reach of children.

Mistletoe has a wide growing range, from Canada to Florida, and as far west as New Mexico. It can be found in China, and in Europe it grows as far south as the Mediterranean. I saw it first in Florida, growing high on trees. I asked a friend, native of the area, how did they harvest it. Did they use some sort of a cherry picker? She replied that her brothers shot it down. This was many years ago, and I suspect that this is no longer allowed.

The name, mistletoe, evokes mists and forest and perhaps the toe-hold it has on the host plant. But this may be misleading. According to some etymologists, in Anglo-Saxon "mistel" means dung, and "tan" means a twig. They called it so because they thought that the plant could not grow on tree branches until the seeds had passed through the digestive system of the birds.

Today we know this is false. The seeds get attached to the host tree when birds accidentally drop the berries, or when they scrape them off their beaks on the bark. Since the berries are sticky, they do not fall off the tree. After a few days they start developing small roots that work their way through the bark into the tree. They grow into round shrubs which stay firmly attached to the branches until someone pulls them or shoots them down.

A final word about mistletoe etiquette. After each kiss one berry should be removed from the bunch. When all berries are gone - no more kisses. So find yourself a big ball of mistletoe with lots of berries.

CAMELS

Camels - I have been thinking about them lately. Christmas is a natural time to think about them, as they are on signs, cards and in mangers with the three kings. But I was thinking mainly how they live and what they eat, and also about their disposition. With camels you always think of their disposition.

In our family's créche we have four splendid camels with their stable boy. They have colorful rugs on their backs and ornate saddles. They look impressive and regal. Which is not how I remember camels. Of course I don't know a huge number of camels, just those I saw along the dusty roads in Morocco and the two we had with us when camping in the Sahara desert. Some of them, especially in the cities, were rather mangy looking.

The other reason I think about camels is our recent dry weather. Looking at the pasture I wonder whether our cows may not be replaced by a herd of camels if it should become as arid here as in the Sahara desert. Camels can survive on very little, water as well as food. The Sahara desert is their pasture. It is not completely barren, there is more to desert than sand, and camels are part of it.

I made the acquaintance of Massoud and Laftiga and their two teenage handlers Naguib and Fatah, while trekking in the Sahara desert. Massoud was a male and Laftiga a female and she was my camel - but only nominally. Camels are uppity, she let me ride her if she felt like it. When she wanted me to dismount she stopped in her tracks, got down on her knees and that was it. I had to walk the rest of the way. Not that I blame her; she and Massoud also had to carry all the gear for the four of us.

A camel saddle is no thing of beauty. It is a rather crude metal contraption which looks like a primitive rocking horse, with flat rockers, and is covered on both sides with blankets. It is attached to the camel's hump so that only a T-shaped holding bar protrudes in the front. The holding bar is useful when the camel kneels down suddenly; it prevents one from plummeting off, head first. To the back and sides are tied various baskets and bundles of provisions. The rider sits on top of it all, swaying with the camel's gait.

We got our camels in a little dusty town, M'Hamid, which is literally at the end of the road. The road which leads there from Quarzazate and Zagora peters out at the edge of sand dunes and the desert. At one time this used to be a departing point for caravans to Timbuktu. The journey took 52 days. We did not take the road to Timbuktu, but some of the merchants still use camels rather than trucks to move their goods across the desert. They say it is cheaper.

Once we left the sand dunes of M'Hamid the ground became rocky, partly because we followed a dry river bed. Sahara is not as sandy as I thought, at least half of the time we hiked over gently rolling but rocky land. And things grew on it. There were bushes with small leaves and sharp thorns, here and there a stand of palms or trees with leathery leaves, and close to the ground grew any number of small plants and flowers. I was amazed how many different plants were thriving there.

For lunch or dinner we stopped at some grove of trees, for the shade. Naguib and Fatah looked around for wood for the cooking fire. Somehow they always found it. After the sun set the air became cold and a fire felt good. Cooking took a long time at least couple of hours resulting in a fragrant, mostly vegetarian, stew called tajin. While we waited we drank Moroccan tea, sweet and minty, served in small cups. One night Fatah baked bread over night in the fire's ashes.

The camels were hobbled so they would not run away, but not tied up because they needed to graze. They had to find their own dinner. I followed them to see what they ate - which was pretty much anything. How they managed to get to the small leaves on the spiky bush is a mystery to me, but they were rather fond of it.

When we came closer to an oasis we also saw camel herds, sometimes several hundred strong. They were graceful animals of many colors, from white to almost black. But I was told that after several years of severe drought it was very difficult, if not impossible, to maintain these herds. And that the local nomads have fallen on hard times. We saw them and visited them in their tents. Besides the camels they also raised goats.

The oasis where we stayed for several days was called D'Oum Laalag and belonged to the Iriqui tribe. The Iriqui wear bright blue flowing robes and blue or black long scarves as turbans or to cover their faces against the desert winds. We too had the scarves to protect us from the blowing sand.

The settlement at the oasis was in sort of a stockade, with tents for people and pens for animals around a big courtyard. It had accommodations for visitors in large cloth tents, and joy of joys, it even had a cold shower. The spring itself was strong, coming from a rock, surrounded by tall date palms and other lush vegetation. The water flowed for about half a mile, forming a small pond, before disappearing into the desert. There was another, smaller spring about a mile away where some nomads camped.

We took hikes to see the dunes, high and rolling far in the distance, to dilapidated forts on hilltops, and to ancient encampments. Our hosts, the Iriqui, were hospitable, arranging the excursions as well as evening entertainment around the fire - native music performed on all sorts of improvised instruments, from a cooking pot and plastic water jerry can, to a string instrument made from a coffee can, piece of wood, and some strings. It sounded pretty good.

Sitting there at night by the fire the world looked like in the days of the three kings, two thousand years ago. And after the fire died you saw the stars, bright and luminous. You could have followed them. We were sad when we had to leave.

THE MAGI

Now when Jesus was born in Bethlehem of Judaea in the days of Herod the king, behold, there came wise men from the east to Jerusalem, saying, "Where is he that is born King of the Jews? for we have seen his star in the east, and are come to worship him." They also brought presents; gold, frankincense and myrrh.

The gift of gold is a natural, but why the other two? There is something mysterious, magical about frankincense and myrrh. What were they? As it turns out they are both products of plants, although not the kind you find at your neighborhood nursery, or grow in your garden. They are both gum resin harvested from semi-tropical trees, similar to pitch from pines and other evergreens.

Frankincense comes from trees of the genus Boswellia that grow in Somalia and South Arabia. Highly fragrant, it is an important ingredient of incense. The ancients used it also in medicine, as an antidote to hemlock, for gangrenous sores, and as treatment of gonorrhea and leprosy, although evidence is lacking about its efficacy. But if it did not help the patients, at least it made them smell good.

To harvest frankincense a deep incision is made in the trunk of the tree, and below it a narrow strip of bark is peeled off. This exudes milk-like juice which in about three months hardens into large clear globules. If lit, it burns with a bright white flame. According to the Latin author Pliny the Elder, an authority on natural history who had an opinion on almost any subject, good frankincense is recognized by its whiteness, size, brittleness and flammability. Less pure resin has a yellowish color. By the way, Pliny's zeal to gather information about the natural world was his undoing. In AD 79 he went to Pompeii to study the volcano Mt. Vesuvius and died in the eruptions which destroyed the city.

Myrrh is also native to northeastern Africa and Saudi Arabia. It is a bushy, spiny tree, growing to 15 feet, with yellow-red flowers and pointed fruit. The gum resin is collected from cuts in the trunk or branches. It dries into brownish lumps. When ground up and mixed with oil or water, myrrh has astringent and anti-inflammatory properties, and it has been used in medicine since the ancient Egyptians. Even today it can be useful as a gargle for mouth and throat problems, or as a salve for canker sores, acne or boils.

The dried gum resin powder can be rubbed into sore gums against gingivitis. A tincture of it makes a good mouthwash, with a drying, slightly bitter taste which clears the sinuses. Externally it will help mild skin problems. Myrrh has also been used in perfumes, incense and in embalming,

Despite their many uses, whether frankincense or myrrh are ideal gifts for a newborn baby is debatable. They are not what babies need. But St. Matthew in his scripture did not go into why the Wise Men brought them. All he said was, "...and when they had opened their treasures, they presented unto him gifts; gold, frankincense, and myrrh." He did not even say how many Wise Men there were. All that came later, the number, their names, and where they came from.

By the second century the Magi were linked with two Old Testament prophecies that kings bearing gifts would come to Israel, and based on that, were elevated to a royal status. By the sixth century Magi and Kings were used interchangeably. The ancient writers originally thought that there were two Wise Men, with others saying there were four, and St. Augustine believed there were twelve of them. In the second century they settled on three, because of the three gifts. One from each.

It was not until the eighth century that the Kings acquired names and nationalities. Melchior was seen as an old man, Balthasar, coming from Ethiopia, somewhat younger, and Gaspar as a young man. The legends about them grew. In the late 14th century these were collected by a monk, John of Hildersheim, into a "Story of the Three Kings." Even earlier, in the 13th century, Jacobus de Voragine wrote about them in "Legenda aurea." And that was only the beginning.

Even the ancients pondered the significance of the gifts, whether they were practical or symbolic. Those who saw them as symbols said that gold meant Christ as King of the world, frankincense was prayer, and myrrh (from a thorny tree) a symbol of Christ's approaching sacrifice. The pragmatic camp saw gold as financial aid to the impoverished Mary, frankincense to ward off stable smells and the myrrh to deter the stable's vermin.

Over the centuries the role of Three Kings in Christmas observations grew. They even got their own holiday. We think of them as arriving at the manger on Christmas Eve. Not so. They came, according to legend, a week later, on January 6, which we celebrate as the Epiphany.

That reminds me of a comment I read somewhere recently. That if instead of Wise Men there had been three Wise Women, they would not have wandered about, but asked for directions, and arrived in time to tidy up the manger, assist with the birth, and they would have brought something practical like diapers and a warm casserole.

VIRTUAL GARDENING

The annual avalanche of garden catalogs is here. Each mail brings more of them, all lovely, all seductive. Some tout plants in their glorious colors, others things which promise to make our gardening easier. These catalogs are supposed to get us out of winter doldrums, dust off our optimism and make us buy. With me it usually works. Dark, short, cold days make me bilious, in need of distraction. So I look, and before I know, I order. I am like Oscar Wilde who said: "I can resist everything except temptation."

But there are limits. It is one thing to order plants, they are real, very much so, something like children or pets. Once they arrive, you cannot ignore them. You have to find a place for them, take care of them. Something else are various gardening tools and gadgets. Gadgets are the bane of our existence. Yes, one needs a proper tool to do a job well, but what makes a proper tool is flexible. A stick or a rock or folded piece of paper can be as good as a fancy trowel, flower bed edging or a seed spreader. It is tempting to think that fancy tools will make us fancy gardeners, but it ain't so, they will probably end up cluttering the garden shed. The same is true in kitchens where gadgets clog up cupboards and drawers. The only absolutely essential cooking tool is a sharp knife. I have one now; it is Japanese, and my life has changed for the better.

But all this pales before a new trend: CD-ROM gardening; that is interactive gardening on computer. I am just looking at a catalog published by the American Nurseryman offering horticultural books, videos and software. In addition to lavishly illustrated books and video cassettes, it is offering a number of gardening computer disks. And I have a problem with that.

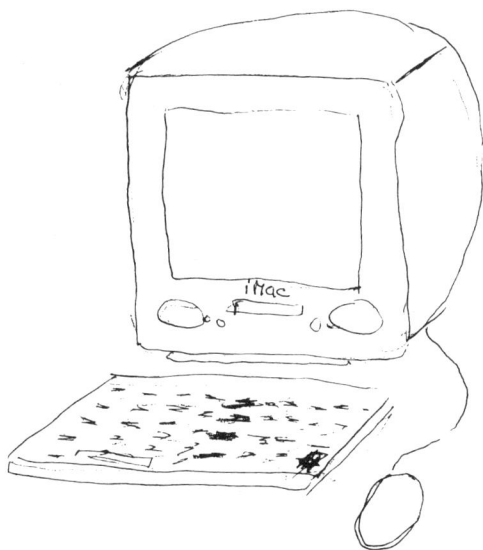

I like garden books; I have many of them myself. I am less fond of anything that has to be viewed on a screen; because one cannot flip through it while sitting on the porch. And CD-ROM disks really bother me. There is no doubt that they contain useful information, but I am concerned about the side effects.

On the positive side, as a reference, CDs have all the bells and whistles. If you have a computer with enough memory and the right program, you can get a 10,000 plant database of trees, shrubs, ground cover, vines, annuals, perennials and ornamental grasses from every section of the U.S. and Canada. To it you can add your own photos and open and edit the database against 500 plant characteristics, and it has more than 4,000 printable and exportable plant images. It will set you back $349.94 not including shipping.

If landscape design is your game, for $495 you may have the LandDesignerPro advertised as the complete, affordable solution for all your design needs. There are other disks, with plant profiles, photo libraries of trees, perennial plants and others, on which you can search for plants by common or scientific name, by family, color and bark, and you can add your own information to the data base.

In fact, there is so much interesting stuff on these disks that you may never leave your computer. You never need to go outside into the garden. The disks have everything, every flower you may want, seen in a variety of stages, effortlessly manipulatable. No more dirt under your fingernails, no more creaky knees and strained backs, insect bites or sunburn; much less the disappointment of having seedlings eaten by slugs.

It is the perfect gardening - virtual gardening. This may be for some people. As they say, "Chaçun a son gout" - which is not "Chaçun's son is suffering from gout," but "Each to his own taste." But I don't like it. I don't want to spend more time sitting at the computer. I like to be outside digging in the dirt. I like the physical part of gardening more than the theoretical. I like the messiness, the uncertainty and the surprises. Virtual is not for me - I like the real stuff.

INDEX

GARDEN THOUGHTS
Marta Kastner
illustrated by Dorothy Blackwell

CEDAR HILL PRESS
1093 Forge Rd.
Lexington, VA, 24450

Copyright 2004 by Marta Kastner

ISBN 0-9637343-1-8

Printed by the News-Gazette Corp.
Lexington, VA